D0021349

the mother in me

the mother in me

*Real-World Reflections
on Growing into Motherhood*

Edited by Kathryn Lynard Soper

Photographs by Maralise Petersen

DESERET
BOOK

Salt Lake City, Utah

The following works were first published in *Segullah: Writings by Latter-day Saint Women*

"Small Sacrifice"
"Ultrasound"
"Finding Myself on Google"
"Blood and Milk"
"Indulgence"
"origami birds"
"Intent to Do Good"
"we all hate to be alone"
"Will It Ever Be Enough?"
"One Eternal Round"
"no time"
"Was Barbie from the Triassic Period?"
"Inheritance"
"Since You Were Born"

"Umbilical Cord" was first published in *Irreantum*

"Encircling" was first published in *Exponent II*

"Wonder Mold Mother" was first published in *Literary Mama*

Compilation © 2008 The Segullah Group, Inc.

Interior photographs © 2008 Maralise Petersen

All rights reserved. No part of this book may be reproduced in any form or by any means without permission in writing from the publisher, Deseret Book Company, P. O. Box 30178, Salt Lake City, Utah 84130. This work is not an official publication of The Church of Jesus Christ of Latter-day Saints. The views expressed herein are the responsibility of the author and do not necessarily represent the position of the Church or of Deseret Book Company.

DESERET BOOK is a registered trademark of Deseret Book Company.

Visit us at DeseretBook.com

Library of Congress Cataloging-in-Publication Data

The mother in me : real-world reflections on growing into motherhood / edited by Kathryn Lynard Soper.
    p.   cm.
   Includes bibliographical references.
   ISBN 978-1-60641-014-1 (hardcover : alk. paper)
  1. Motherhood—Religious aspects—Mormon Church.   2. Mormon women—Religious life.   I. Soper, Kathryn Lynard.
   BX8641.M68 2008
   242'.6431—dc22   2008016071

Printed in the United States of America
Sheridan Books, Chelsea, MI

10 9 8 7 6 5 4 3 2 1

*To our mothers
and our children*

Contents

Editor's Acknowledgments xi

Foreword *by Beverly Campbell* xiii

Introduction: Beginning *by Kathryn Lynard Soper* 1

1. Forty Weeks 'Til Spring
   by Johanna Buchert Smith 9

2. Umbilical Cord *by Darlene Young* 25

3. Angel Mother *by Angela W. Schultz* 26

4. Expectations *by Kristen Ridge* 34

5. Given and Giver *by Darlene Young* 43

6. They Weren't Mine to Keep
   by Melonie Cannon 45

7. The Yoke of Wisdom *by Melissa Young* 59

8. Encircling *by Kylie Turley* 65

9. Small Sacrifice *by Lani B. Whitney* 67

10. Ultrasound *by Emily Milner* 71

11. Finding Myself on Google *by Emily Milner* 72

12. Blood and Milk *by Sharlee Mullins Glenn* 83

13. Giraffes Kiss *by Heather Harris Bergevin* 85

Contents

14. 3 A.M. *by Heather Harris Bergevin* 96

15. Grace and Glorie *by Lisa Meadows Garfield* 98

16. Indulgence *by Heather Herrick* 108

17. Earthbound *by Brittney Poulsen Carman* 109

18. origami birds *by Johnna Benson Cornett* 115

19. The Tree of Life *by Megan Aikele Davies* 117

20. Intent to Do Good *by Ailene Long* 128

21. Ice and Fire *by Melissa Young* 133

22. Creation out of Chaos *by Heather Herrick* 134

23. no time *by Johnna Benson Cornett* 142

24. Natural-Born Mother *by Maralise Petersen* 143

25. we all hate to be alone
    by Johnna Benson Cornett 151

26. Will It Ever Be Enough? *by Felicia Hanosek* 153

27. One Eternal Round *by Lani B. Whitney* 159

28. Strolling with Toddlers *by Jennifer Boyack* 160

29. The Catalogue Children
    by Heather Harris Bergevin 167

30. Was Barbie from the Triassic Period?
    by Justine Clarice Dorton 169

31. That One in the Middle *by Brooke Olsen Benton* 175

32. Big Brother *by Darlene Young* 181

33. Tea Party Blessings *by Heather Oman* 183

34. The Measure of a Mother *by Kylie Turley* 194

35. Inheritance *by Darlene Young* 204

36. Going Up the Mountain *by Allyson Smith* 205

37. East of the Sun, West of the Moon
    by Melonie Cannon 213

38. Wonder Mold Mother *by Lisa Hardman* 215

39. Since You Were Born *by Darlene Young* 226

40. Making the Grass Greener
    by Courtney Kendrick 228

41. Release *by Heather Harris Bergevin* 233

42. Watch with Me *by Emily Halverson* 234

43. April 1996 *by Sharlee Mullins Glenn* 245

About the Authors 248

About the Editor 256

Editor's Acknowledgments

This anthology was created by the editorial staff of *Segullah: Writings by Latter-day Saint Women*. I'm deeply grateful to each of the contributing authors for sharing their beautiful prose and poetry, and to their respective families for supporting their writing efforts. Special thanks go to my husband, Reed, and our seven children for cheering me on throughout the editorial process.

Several individuals merit thanks for other contributions to the anthology. Melissa Young and Emily Halverson provided valuable editorial assistance. Maralise Petersen photographed the stunning mother-and-child images featured in the book. Jana Erickson and Lisa Mangum at Deseret Book gave helpful professional guidance, and Heidi Greenhalgh penned the book's title.

Finally, I thank the founding members of The Segullah Group for sustaining the journal throughout its fledgling years and enabling our organization to blossom. And most importantly, I thank the many women who read and enjoy *Segullah*. Their enthusiasm for candid, insightful, uplifting personal writing by Latter-day Saint women inspired us to create this book.

Foreword

Have you ever pondered those moments that give purpose, meaning, and color to your life?

I have. Especially now, as a mother of four and a grandmother of six, I find myself looking backward over the years, reflecting on the times of greatest significance. My memories overflow with noteworthy challenges, exceptional experiences, immense losses, steadying trials, and unexpected honors. And in this rich array of experiences, none is more meaningful than the time I spent mothering my small children.

As a beginning mother, I wasn't prepared for the awesome reverence I felt for each new life. Nor was I prepared for the flood of emotions that swept over me as I began my journey of discovery. First came the cradling and adoring and kissing, as I admired and caressed every inch of my babies' bodies. Next came the marveling at the way their bodies fit perfectly into the curve of my arm, the flawlessness of tiny fingernails and toes, the curves of diminutive legs and arms, the sweetness found at the napes of their necks, the wisdom of ages emanating from their eyes.

As the weeks went by, I was awed that their little bodies

knew exactly what they needed to do to develop—stretching, kicking, reaching out, and reaching up—always reaching up. I had expected my children to capture my heart and occupy my mind, but I was surprised to find them possessing my whole soul—completely, unequivocally. Like all mothers, I was sure my children were exceptional in every way.

The ensuing years brought similar love and pride, along with the discovery that parenting is hard work—really hard work. Motherhood was sometimes worrisome, sometimes maddening, sometimes tedious, and sometimes lonely, but never insignificant. I learned that an undertaking of such consequence required absolute commitment to the task at hand and an abundance of endurance. I remember many days when just keeping the children all fed, clean, and warm seemed an unattainable goal.

An older friend once counseled me that I should *enjoy* every moment of these years because they would fly by as though in a twinkling. It was true. I turned around and my children were grown—and I wished that I had been more available, more loving, more wise, more spiritual. Even now, I wish I had found more time for the park or the playground. I wish I had rolled on the fresh-cut grass with them or let them set up their tents in the living room more often. I wish they'd seen me laugh and pray and cry more. I wish I'd borne my testimony to them more. I wish—I wish—I wish—but I cannot go back. We can never go back.

Despite my wistfulness, I do not sorrow over those years. On the contrary, I rejoice in the time we shared. I rejoice in the laughter and just plain fun we had together. I even rejoice in the trials that made us who we are—stronger, more committed to each other and to our faith. Indeed, the significant moments of my life have one core: my children, their father, our home, and the covenants we've made which will keep us together until the end of time. These moments are etched indelibly on my soul.

You hold a brilliant book filled with real-life stories of mothers having such moments with their young children. Their accounts will make you laugh and weep and want to reach out, holding tightly the little ones in your life. Their shared experiences will give other mothers strength to go on. They remind me that mothers of today are extraordinary, inclined to do a superior job under greater challenges than did their own mothers.

Mothers of young children, read this collection for yourselves; grandmothers, give it to your daughters and granddaughters. And as you peruse its pages, ponder those significant moments etched into your souls—and consider recording them. We cannot get those moments back, but we can hold on to them with words, making them as eternal as the relationships we so cherish.

Beverly Campbell
Sun Lakes, Arizona

Introduction: Beginning

I lazed in half-sleep, my lower body cocooned in tingling warmth, when the squeezing began—deep and strong. It spread across my abdomen and wrapped around my back, then clamped hard like a tourniquet, forcing my belly upward in a tight ball. For the first time since labor had begun, it hurt.

I rang for the nurse. "I think my epidural's wearing off," I said.

She appeared quickly to check my progress. After a few seconds, she looked at me with a knowing smile. "You're complete," she said. "Ten centimeters. You can start pushing now."

I looked at my husband, Reed, incredulous. After nine months of waiting and watching, nine months of planning and worrying and dreaming, I was surprised to find myself here, on a birthing bed, ready to deliver my firstborn child. On some irrational level, I had thought my pregnancy would never end.

The nurse helped me roll from my side to my back, then raised the head of the bed. "Hold your knees," she said. I tried, but I was shaking with anticipation and couldn't keep my grip. Reed stepped close to help and started cracking corny jokes, the kind that are funny only at the very end of a long night, or a long pregnancy. As my stomach muscles shook with laughter, the pressure began to build again, gathering, rising, then arching to a crest.

Over the next hour, wave after powerful wave passed through me, each one pushing my daughter a little closer to earth. Finally, the birthing was complete. I stared at the baby wriggling on the sterile, blue sheeting, her skin bright and fresh and full of light. None of the birth stories I'd heard prepared me for this shocking discovery: the baby was *alive*. She was moving, breathing, blinking. Without batteries! Without wires or plugs! I had been so consumed with pregnancy that I hadn't really considered the result: a tiny, miraculous human being. A new life had begun for my child. As I cradled her against my chest, I sensed a new life beginning for me as well.

The next few days and weeks proved more exhausting—and exhilarating—than I ever could have imagined. Through trial and error I learned how to breastfeed, clip itty-bitty fingernails, and shampoo a head other than my own. I proved myself capable of getting out of bed at 2 A.M., feeding someone else before I fed myself, and wiping another's bottom without recoiling in disgust. The hours passed in a blur, supersaturated with emotion: bold pride and fierce protectiveness, fear and self-doubt, tenderness so deep it hurt. I never knew my body could give so much; I never knew my heart could feel so much. And I was awestruck by my new role. For twenty-one years I had been a child, a student; now I was a mother, a teacher. I had hopped the fence into adulthood, and I was overcome by the thrills and demands of reinventing myself, of finding the mother in me.

It was tough at first. The constant needs of my daughter pushed me to my limits physically, emotionally, and spiritually. But by the time Elizabeth had moved beyond early infancy, I found my groove. I knew what she needed and how to give it to her—and I delighted in doing so. Content and confident, I envisioned myself sailing through the coming years with ease (insert guffaws here). But before long I made another shocking discovery: Elizabeth wouldn't remain a baby for long. She was constantly growing, changing, reaching new milestones—and I needed to keep pace with her. Although I was technically an adult, I had just begun to grow up.

Sixteen months after Elizabeth's birth, we welcomed a son into our family. Benjamin arrived on a frigid December morning. Red-faced and squalling, he quickly upended life as we knew it. I felt as if I were starting motherhood all over again, now having to figure out how to divide myself between two people who wanted all of me. And just when I thought I had things sorted out, things changed again. Potty-training and preschool. Moving from an apartment to a starter home. Welcoming a third baby, then a fourth, then a fifth. New friends. New teachers. New problems. New accomplishments. We bought a family-sized home and welcomed baby number six. In the midst of our happy-yet-crazy family life, I clung to the hope that there was a finish line somewhere, a point at which I'd have everything figured out.

But after our seventh child was diagnosed with Down syndrome, I gave up that delusion. Motherhood, I now know, means continual rounds of beginning.

Today Elizabeth is fifteen; Thomas is three. He'll probably be the last child to join our family. As he becomes increasingly mobile, I realize I'm experiencing yet another beginning: the beginning of the end. Not the end of growth and change—that will continue forever—but the end of this chapter in my life. The end of diapers, sippy cups, Fisher-Price. The end of tricycles and Play-Doh and a hundred other tokens of early childhood. My years of mothering young children are almost over.

I confess, there have been plenty of days I've *wished* for these years to be over. I've longed for solo trips to the grocery store and the bathroom, nights of unbroken sleep, and the chance to sit down and enjoy a meal from start to finish. I have already made plans for what I'll do after dropping

Thomas off for his first day of preschool. (Here's one version: I speed back to the empty house, enter with a triumphant shout, then proceed to crank up the stereo way too loud and eat way too many Oreos. Alone.)

More than once I've had to restrain myself from rolling my eyes at some middle-aged grandma telling me, "Enjoy them while they're young, dear. It goes so fast." In those moments, standing with a baby over my elbow and a toddler tugging my arm and a preschooler whining at my heels, I've been tempted to hand over my brood and say, "Here. *You* enjoy."

But despite my periodic fantasies of life without young children, I can say with complete sincerity that I wouldn't trade these years for anything. Not for the PhD I once dreamed of earning. Not for the writing career that could have been mine. Not for money or travel or a stunning home or a decent wardrobe or anything else I could've enjoyed these past fourteen years if I hadn't chosen to be a mother.

Yes, mothering is hard—harder than any other work I could've chosen. I've invested milk and tears, blood and muscle. Spent thousands and thousands of days feeding, cleaning, rocking, carrying, and teaching. I've given much. But I have received more—far more. I've been given a life worth living, a self worth being. And I have seven children I love more than life, more than self.

In this spirit, I'm pleased to present this volume of poetry and prose, *The Mother in Me.* I'm excited to introduce you to its contributing authors, a group of friends and fellow writers who value motherhood as much as I do. We work together on the staff of *Segullah,* a journal of writings by and for Latter-day Saint women. We believe personal writing is a powerful vehicle for growth, for writers and readers alike. In this anthology, we offer the realities of mothering young children, from pregnancy through kindergarten. Our purpose here is to celebrate this season, to illustrate its unique challenges and delights, to reveal its deep significance.

Let's face it: on those days when we do nothing but wipe bottoms and cook Ramen noodles, significance can be hard to find.

But it's here.

It's here in the details of our days, and it's here in the pages of this book. Some of these writings are humorous, some thoughtful, some poignant—yet each proves that motherhood matters. Not just in the sentimental ways we talk about on Mother's Day, but in the gritty, lovely, everyday realities of walking this path. In these writings we look at the miracles of pregnancy, birth, and adoption; the sorrows of infertility, miscarriage, and stillbirth. We smile and groan over toddler antics and preschooler adventures. We speak frankly about health crises, identity crises, and sanity crises.

And we discover the fruits which come from such struggles: insights gained, hearts expanded, faith increased.

In short, we delve into the messy richness of the domestic realm and find great beauty and meaning therein. For home is where everything begins—for children *and* for mothers.

We're happy you're here to laugh, cry, think, and rejoice with us. To fellow mothers, we offer our companionship. To future mothers, we offer a warm invitation to join us in due time. We don't know exactly what awaits you in this wild and wondrous realm, but we can promise you this: you'll meet unprecedented challenges and enjoy unspeakable blessings as you discover the mother in you.

Kathryn Lynard Soper
South Jordan, Utah

Forty Weeks 'Til Spring

Johanna Buchert Smith

AUGUST

The birds are quiet these mornings; our orchard in the back is full of them. I've found a robin's nest built solidly between two crossing branches on an early-bearing apple. Yellow-fleshed with pink cheeks, these summer apples were partly why I fell in love with our house, though right now, even a ripe, pink apple holds zero appeal.

Actually, I've never liked the color, but last month two pale stripes of it showed up on a pregnancy test, and pink became very personal. Mostly now, I try not to feel green as I make myself wake up, stand up, and walk our dog, Duke, up the Gibson Jack, the National Forest trail near our house. Backlit in clumps, every blade of field grass is a luminous stained-glass window, and just before dusk, the trail is ablaze as though guarded with a flaming sword.

When I woke from my nap yesterday, the sunlight coming in the kitchen had turned a deep, reddish orange. Outside a huge column of smoke looked to be coming from right up the canyon. I called the police, who told me the fire was east of our town on the Reservation, that they were controlling it. With my constantly uneasy middle, I took a long time putting on my clothes, socks, and shoes, and getting my body outside. Duke pulled me the entire mile to the trailhead as if I were a sleigh. Every once in a while, I had to stop and squat on the pavement to let the sour in my stomach subside a bit. Whenever I'm not sitting or lying down, I'm trapped in the just-shy-of-mouth-watering stage of nausea.

The huge, sun-choking smoke column was clearly visible all the way up the hill. Once at the trailhead, I sat by the water for a while, reaching in and dropping handfuls of water on my arms. I felt prickly and sticky with heat. I was emphatically *not* holding my gut in, and it protruded as if I were five months along. Or what I thought I would look like at five months pregnant.

This is my first pregnancy—my first *everything*, it feels like. I wonder vaguely if Eve ever felt as I do. On some theoretical level I know I wanted this—even chose it—but did even Eve pause in her purposefulness when she realized the known world of her peaceful garden was now nonexistent, that in choosing family, she chose to become part of the wildness of creation?

Only in my secret heart of hearts have I allowed myself to dream and hope for motherhood. I wanted to be sure I was "ready," that I would have all my bad habits eliminated and all the good ones that I've been trying to form firmly established. Now because of this tiny cluster of cells that are growing another human, I feel the thick, unruliness of the whole thing, like the fire up the canyon. It fills me with uneasiness, a sense of dread. What if *I* am consumed? What if this leaves me charred and black, as thin and bare and powerless as a juniper after a brush fire?

It's silly, but I notice I'm trying to dupe myself into pretending nothing is happening. There's nothing different about this coming fall. *Nothing* different, I tell myself. I do *not* feel like throwing up at the thought of food or of getting into a hot car, or the sound of boring conversations. I have *utmost* patience for the sound of Duke licking himself, and, no, it does *not* send me into irrational rage. I do *not* feel as though I just ate an undercooked hamburger every time I stand up. And it's perfectly normal to be brought to tears by the beauty of my sweetheart, Andy, or the tender strains of "Pie Jesu."

Right?

Today I woke up in the middle of the night to a house full of wood smoke; the winds had shifted, bringing the fire smell directly to our bedroom. It's really strong, that end-of-the-fire smothery odor. Eyes closed, I lie in bed, desperate to not notice the cloudy smoldering I feel in every cell of my body, desperate to ignore these smoky winds of permanent change that have blown through our open windows.

SEPTEMBER

Up until now I've been in denial, not because I'm not pretty much delighted when I look at the big picture, but because my day-to-day sense has been much more one of terror. And not about the flesh-tearing eventuality of this growth, but because of just plain change, and being stuck with it. I feel like I've scaled to the top of a cliff, and there's no way down except to jump.

But I'm Options Girl! Even if I know all along the one door I want to open, I feel much better when I know that *just in case* I change my mind, I have another door to escape through.

I've been so clumsy around the words of the experience, carefully keeping it at a distance with impersonal pronouns— it's still "a" or "this" baby—and even hypothetical, as in, "if we have a baby." Just using the word *baby* feels like an enormous commitment. Part of this is because I get kind of grossed out when I think about a living creature inside me. It's almost like having worms or something. And this creature will eventually crawl out of me and feed off me. It's just so strange.

But today the phrase *little lima bean* keeps reverberating between my ears, and I wonder how big, if it really is there, the baby in me might be. I go to the Nova website and look at developing baby pictures. Oh, I've already missed most of the show. This thing inside me has not just arms and legs, but separated fingers and toes and ears by now! Supposedly it can scrunch its eyebrows. Purse its lips. (It is so odd to think of another pair of eyebrows swimming around in my pelvic region.) It really looks like a baby, not just a soft bug you'd find underwater. I'm growing a real-live little human.

That's a relief, you know. When Andy and I first got married, I was convinced for a long time that if we had a baby it would be a monster, not a person. I'm not sure where this stemmed from; it wasn't something as logical as genetics. I just didn't think it was possible that something soft and pink and sweet would come from me. Really, the thought terrified me. I wondered if it was even fair for us to create a body for some little spirit.

So I'm making today the turning point: from now on it is *our baby*, or *my baby*, or *her*, not "it." And she's no longer hypothetical; she's already here, finishing up growing from the inside out. I will not freak out or involuntarily cringe or quiver at the word "mama," and I will take ownership in a way that reflects how much I've wanted this for a long time.

Andy sweetly reassures me, "You were born to be a mom!" Born or made, it's what I am now.

OCTOBER

Today I see the loveliest thing I've seen in a good long while: the white-wrapped egg sack of a mama hobo spider.

I've seen lots of them while moving stones this summer, but haven't taken time to truly inspect one. This time I get the Exacto knife out of the tool bucket and ruthlessly slice it open. The insides are surprisingly benign (no leaping, lethal bite-o'-death chompers), beautifully intricate and delicate.

The first layer is a smooth, white silk tarp attaching the round sack to the log. The lumpiness under it that I was so hesitant of is only a protective, insulating coat of mud bits and sawdust pieces. Under that is a much thicker, smaller ball of deep, spun silk, and finally, inside that are fifty or sixty dry, pearlescent, roly little eggs the size of poppy seeds.

They're beautiful. With their cocooning removed, they spill all over the log, rolling until they find little cracks to perch in. Though I try slicing open one of the eggs, the razor is much too coarse an instrument, and I only succeed in juicily squishing one egg one after another. I'm amazed when I think that these little eggs laid in October will hatch out in June. Reproduction is just one miracle after another.

Our household reproduction is due to hatch out in April. So I learned a few weeks ago at my first checkup. That was a milestone. I had looked forward to it like it would be some kind of holiday, instead of what it actually was—a physical. Andy had taken the morning off work, and though it was a little odd at first to have him in the examination room (only because I've never had a breast and pelvic exam with company before), the whole thing turned out to be a magnificent experience.

Tracy, the nurse-midwife, pushed up my uterus with her fingers and let us both feel it, round and the size of an orange, then put the Doppler up to it. We heard a magical woosha-woosha-woosha little heartbeat. Andy and I both burst into tears and started laughing. He handed me tissues, and I tried to keep my stomach still long enough for Tracy to hear a good count. I'd take however many blood draws they wanted if it meant I could hear that.

Andy and I congratulated each other the rest of the morning and lunched out for soup and sandwiches. While we gnawed our pickles, an enormous clap of thunder and a fireball hit the sidewalk right outside the window, shaking us in our seats. Everyone in the café ran out to see if a sign had come crashing down.

No sign lay on the pavement, but signs for me were everywhere else: unstoppable, unusual, pouring rain, and a fireball thundering from my belly that might shake us in our seats.

NOVEMBER

The stillness of snow will do one of two things to me: yank joyful shouts from my throat and get my arms and legs swinging and skidding, or it will hush me, like it has the chickadees and clattery cotoneaster bush and the bearded wheatgrass.

On Thanksgiving weekend, the sky dropped a solid two feet of snow all at once, brought a quiet finger to its white lips and shushed the whole world around us. We didn't realize until later that we'd seen the last of our dark soil until spring. But it's more than soil disappearing. It's also my last carefree run. My last great night's sleep. These days I sleep packed in soft white mounds of pillows, as though I were outside in that quiet, white world.

As though *I* am the dark soil, dormant forty weeks till spring, harboring a spring bulb under layers of pale skin.

DECEMBER

Third anniversary. Andy gets up to go to work in winter black at 4:00 A.M. so he can be done early enough for us to do something fun this evening. My afternoon at the spa, courtesy of a gift certificate and a couple of coupons, is mysterously a fiasco. Andy meets me there, and I'm in unstoppable tears as soon as I'm out the door. We're both confused. Am I really as huge as I feel? At six feet, even I'm surprised that there's anything fragile about me.

But as my excitement for this little sprout increases, I become less and less sure of my capacity to add the role of "mother" to that of "wife." It's like trying to be more than one planet in a single universe.

We drive an hour to eat Thai food and watch the new *Pride and Prejudice*. I wish for Tums, and wonder where my taste for strong flavors went. We find the movie theatre with barely enough time to be seated, then decide we'd rather be home snuggled up and going to bed than watching this movie and getting home late. We drive back home.

In bed, I suddenly feel a commotion in the hard ball where my girl, Scout, lives. I flatten my hand on her and not only feel her moving unmistakably from the inside out, but from the outside in. A poke swings across my belly like a shooting star.

January

When this pregnancy began, my sister Heidi cautioned, "Suddenly you'll find that you've turned into Mama Bear."

That moment has arrived. I felt the first growly beginnings as I contemplated the photograph the ultrasound tech sent home with us, the streaky glimpse through my skin at our flowering blossom labeled "baby girl."

I don't object to knowing the baby's sex. For the last five months, Andy and I wanted to be surprised, but three days before the ultrasound appointment, we decided we'd take a little peek, so that we could be surprised sooner. I even drank myself to near-incontinence so we'd have a "clear window." Stretched out on the table, I peeled my shirt and paneled pants off my belly and only flinched a little when I got squirted and smeared with the cold lubricant.

"There's no mistaking *that,*" the tech told us briskly, referring to an absence as we gazed up through two peanut-shaped femurs. Without a pause she moved on to photograph the baby's little feet, her shapely leg, her sweet profile, her delicate arm and fingers.

Certainly I don't object to the clinician previewing everything from nose formation to heart chamber count to that little bum Andy will be tenderly swabbing for the next few years. But it's another matter entirely to print out the image for the entire world to stare at. We will leave this child some dignity; that "baby girl" picture will be tucked safely away to protect her privacy.

I am Mama Bear, hear me roar!

True, I'd gotten crotchety about daughter-related issues plenty of times before: *she shall not live in a pink zone; she shall not be a dolly girl.* But those grumbles hadn't come from Mama Bear. They came from Just Plain Joh, reliving her own girlhood and declaring that *this* baby must follow suit. Mama Bear knows better.

There is nothing superficial about this fierceness fueled by love rather than preference, nor about the great and terrible Mama Bear protector I'm becoming as I grow this child within me.

The funny thing about becoming a Mama Bear is that you suddenly realize you've been living in the center of a whole tribe of Mama Bears forever and never knew it.

FEBRUARY

This is the bitter dregs of winter, the month everybody loves to hate. Raw winds still whip snow in meager, frozen drifts, and nighttime temperatures harden any south-facing slope that even *thinks* of softening. But if you're observant, you'll notice February is also a month of loosening and swelling.

The dogwood by the creek is coloring a deep magenta. Tiny, hard tree buds are now clearly visible on every slender twig. The sun is climbing higher—it's light out until six—and the snow even melts in the afternoon. Leaves, pieces of bark, and other dark bits of detritus that have collected on the snow's surface over the winter act as tiny solar collectors, drilling shafts deep into the snow. Life is, incredibly, leaping forward.

The familiarity of the life leaping inside me is now a comfort. Was it really only six months ago that I felt such a mixture of apprehension and distrust of this process? That I was afraid of being taken over by pregnancy? In fact, the regularity of tapping hiccups and poking legs has become the metronome of my day.

At first I wasn't sure what I was feeling. When Heidi was

pregnant with her first, she introduced me to a whole vocabulary. For the most part, I was either grossed out by the gooeyness of it (*stripping the membranes, bloody show*) or bugged by the male presence in it (*Braxton Hicks, Kegels*).

I thought this girl had gotten really good at poking out all her bony parts at once—elbows, knees, little bum and back—so that everything felt hard at once. Then Tracy asked if I'd had any Braxton Hicks contractions yet. The name of these practice contractions no longer strikes me as an obtrusive, male obstetric term. It's more like an endearing nickname for what happens when this melon-belly of mine grows a hard rind for a few seconds.

Whether or not the ground is softening, *I* am. It's incredibly powerful to see my body transforming so capably, and it gives me hope that in fluid synchronicity, my mind and heart and spirit are also growing. I may be capable of motherhood after all. The earth and I have been in stolid dormancy, but many kinds of life will soon spring forth from us both.

MARCH

Now that the trail has dried out some, I've resumed my walks up Gibson Jack. These last weeks, in contrast to my canyon hikes, which have slowed to rambles, the landmarks of pregnancy that every book has me watching for have accelerated. The incontinence. The jumpy legs. The heartburn.

The sciatic pain that collapses me as though someone has knocked my knees out from behind.

And then there's the appearance of colostrum. I heartily reject *What To Expect*'s description as "thin, yellowish discharge." Look, can we agree to not call anything as perfect as breast milk *discharge?* You wouldn't ask someone to pick up a gallon of "thin, whitish cow's discharge" on the way home from work, would you? Besides, I'd hardly describe the stuff I produce as *yellowish.* School-bus orange would be more to the point—colostrum concentrate.

Living in the bright intermountain desert, I savor every cloudy moment. This month's thick, pendulous clouds foretell impending thunderstorms. And more than that. March's rain is a forecast for the rest of the summer. Combined with winter run-off from snow in the mountains, the rain fills the streams, replenishes aquifers, and restores reservoirs. The storms of March nurture the rest of the year.

Colostrum is my spring storm ensuring summer growth. This pregnancy, like this spring, will be over soon, but I'll continue to nurture this life as it keeps growing. It is colostrum, of all things, that shows me my future: not only can I create and grow life, I can sustain it. I have the cloudy, slipping thought that perhaps this is the essence of motherhood—feeding, nourishing.

Which is why that first tiny drop, of all the changes to my

body, might have been the thing that felt most deserving of a celebration. Where's my white gown, my mariachi band, my crown and bouquet? The appearance of colostrum is an announcement, a declaration of independence, an official notification about my own body to myself: I am a woman now.

APRIL

The boredom of restrained anticipation set in about three weeks ago. The same fully focused energy that went into making sure I ate right, drank enough, and exercised well is now bent to forgetting that I'm waiting—oh, interminably waiting!

Echoing the finches and thrushes in the orchard, I fully surrendered to my need to fluff pillows and make soft places, to order and reorder our home.

Now Scout's due date has come and gone. I'm impatient, I'm excited, and I'm out in the garden making raised beds. (*Oh, where are you, Scout?*) My taut body moves the rake through piles of last year's leaves, and the sun feels heavenly warm on my bent back. In ballooned shadow, the other side of me holds another, but tiny, divine light.

Though, frankly she doesn't seem so tiny right now. I'm out here so often that Andy keeps joking I'm going to deliver in the compost pile. I pause to squat every few minutes (*We can't wait to meet you, love. Are you coming?),* doubled over and leaning on my rake.

But I've soaked up enough confidence about delivery that any speck of fear I felt before has melted in the spring warmth. *(Come on out, my dear. Don't be afraid.)* The crazy thing about pregnancy (and it's the same thing that's crazy about love, pain, and death) is that it has the peculiarity of being the most personal experience at the same time as being one of the most universal.

Only something as enduring as an archetype will suffice as a description, but never could an archetype explain how personalized and intimate this experience is. And like the arrival of any new season—like any of the most significant changes in nature—it has occurred by almost imperceptible degrees. I've grown this mountain of a belly, and the frozen lake of hesitation that my heart beat in a mere forty weeks ago is now a brilliant, warm pool of anticipation.

MAY

Scout Madeleine was born on a Friday night at the end of April. It was the most magnificent teamwork I've ever been part of. Andy applied counter pressure and never left my side. My incredible midwives kept me laughing and fed me shredded ice. My mum read from *To Kill a Mockingbird* between contractions, at least at first. And in the final act,

Scout latched on to my breast with a ferocious intensity, as hungry for me as I've been for her.

Now that I'm home with this little crumb of freshness, I feel thin and translucent, like I've been rolled out over my entire world with a rolling pin, and simultaneously feel bunched up in a warm firm ball around this tiny girl. My lips hardly stray from her wonderfully scented scalp; my nose nuzzles every inch of her whipped-cream skin. Her tiny fists slowly unfurl, like fiddleheads in May.

It's cliché, it's impossible, but it really does seem as though this year's spring is just for us. Gossamer-winged spring azures line the Gibson Jack trail and flutter around my feet, as though creating a royal welcome path for this mama and babe. I hold her close, alert and bundled, and wander out into our full-bloom orchard in my nightgown. Robins, orioles, finches, juncos, meadowlarks, and magpies fill the air with bright family calling. Wisps of yellow powder twist and flutter in the breeze off the Austrian pine at the bottom of the front yard, pollinating the world.

This is a holy time. Like Eve, I've discovered the Earth again on this seventh day: everything is fresh, alive, vibrant and new, beautiful and wonderful and created for me and my daughter. Everything is reproducing after its own kind—and now I know just how good it really is.

Umbilical Cord

Darlene Young

Yes, press your hand against my flesh to feel
This fresh-bright life, this future man of God
Flex tiny stretching legs to test the walls
Of a quart-sized world of warm and wet.

All life he drinks direct through twisted cord,
Source of constant nourishment through me;
Fast it holds, despite his testing squirms,
Building a defense from future harm.

There! Your palm is humming from his kick
But now you move away and fall asleep . . .

Soon your hands will press against his head
While I pray empty-bellied on a pew,
Flesh on flesh, you'll make the cord of life—
Antibody strength for future fights;

May it hold fast.

Angel Mother

Angela W. Schultz

I throw the book aside and stomp tearfully into the bathroom. I'm looking for encouragement, not reminders of my
own inadequacy, yet despite my attempt to escape the words
on the page, they play again and again in my mind—*angel
mother.* The term used by a prophet of God to describe his
own. Maybe on another day, when I've slept more, when the
children fight less, when I'm not straining against the physical and emotional challenges of preparing for yet another
birth, I could read those words without criticizing my own
mothering efforts. Perhaps I would even find them
inspirational.

But not today.

I think for a moment about my own humble beginnings
as a full-time mother. I resisted that role for a full two years
after my eldest daughter was born. Our family's discussion
of the matter was brief and to the point. Wading through the
piles of papers and clothes on my office floor to find me at
my desk, my husband said to me, "I'd better stay home with
the baby. If you do it, I'm afraid that at the end of the day,
I'll find you sitting naked, absorbed in a pile of books and

newspapers, with the baby eating out of the cat box in the other room."

I wasn't offended; he had a point.

Homemaking wasn't my strength. Assertive, outspoken, and opinionated, I thrived on the mental stimulation and competition I found in academic and career pursuits. I finished high school in three years as a National Merit Scholar and went on to complete my bachelor's degree—with honors—in two years while married and working. I was just wrapping up my master's degree when motherhood came knocking. I had no idea then that homemaking offers its own exhilarating challenges and breathtaking rewards. Since we weren't religious, I felt no special obligation to become a stay-at-home mother. I did consider it important for my daughter to have a consistent caregiver to bond with. It just never occurred to me that that caregiver should be me.

So for the first two years of my daughter's life, my husband was her primary caregiver. I went to work every morning while Don sang nursery rhymes, changed diapers, and cooked meals at home. When we went out, he carried our daughter in a baby sling.

"Good for you," people told me. "You already carried that baby for nine months. It's his turn."

The problem is, it didn't work. Oh, Don was a good homemaker. Our house was always orderly and peaceful, and he took excellent care of McKinley. But she and I both knew who the real mother was. McKinley wanted to nurse every moment I was home—day or night. And as much as I loved my job, I missed her too.

I hung pictures of her on every wall of my office, and I found myself taking long lunches so that I could go home to visit her. All the time I told myself it should be as easy for me to leave her in the morning as it seemed to be for the men in the office to leave their children. But it never was.

As I tried to make sense of this new reality that didn't fit any of my expectations, I found myself terrified by what it meant—the potential disruption not just to the lifestyle I had established, but to my own self-concept. Could it be that everything I had believed about myself was wrong? That all the time and effort invested in school and work was mis-guided? And if I had been wrong about such basic issues in my personal life, in what other ways might I be mistaken?

The sound of so many unanswered questions was deafening.

Eventually I began spending my free time with friends or locked away in my office instead of with Don and McKinley. In a frantic effort to drown out the sound of McKinley's baby laughter, I learned Reiki, reprogrammed my retinal patterns, danced to the goddess at the solstice, and meditated on my past lives.

None of it helped.

In the meantime, my marriage deteriorated almost beyond recognition. Don, the man who I had joyfully eloped with a few years before, moved out of our bedroom. Despite many hours of heartfelt conversation, neither of us could find words to explain what had gone wrong between us—or what might help to make it better. We began instead to discuss the possibility of divorce.

The answer came softly, rippling at the fringes of my consciousness: "Come home."

It was an easy enough thing to discount. After all, modern women are no longer expected to live by outdated stereotypes, are they?

"Come home."

Of the two of us, I was clearly better prepared to support the family. Hadn't I just finished graduate school?

"Come home."

What about my total lack of interest or aptitude in homemaking?

"Come home."

It was Don who finally spoke the words. "Angie, I know this sounds crazy, but I've been having some strong feelings that there *is* something that will help our family. I need to get a full-time job. And it's time for you to come home." The truth hung between us in the air, as tangible as another person joining the conversation. Suddenly there was nothing else to say, nothing further to argue.

Despite my fears, I became a full-time mother.

I approached my new assignment with all of the deliberate focus my years in the world of work had taught me. I wrote myself a mission statement and daily, weekly, monthly, and yearly objectives. I listed the precise intervals that would elapse between days when I cleaned out the cupboards and when I rinsed the garbage cans with bleach. I filled my planner with random events like trips to the second-hand clothing store to shop for items I didn't need—anything to make sure I scheduled every terrifying unstructured hour between the time Don left for work and the time he returned.

When he found me overwhelmed at the end of the day, he gently coached, "You'll feel better with less clutter. Let's start by putting things away. It helps to have different music. Let's light a candle for atmosphere." He showed me where to shop for the best deals on groceries, taught me to plan ahead and stock up on essentials. When dinner didn't come off as well as I'd hoped, he coached me on what flavors and textures might better complement each other. My abilities slowly improved.

But because our decision to return to traditional family roles was quickly followed by a conversion to the gospel, I also had other tasks to master. Becoming a Mormon woman is no small thing. To me it entailed a cultural shift far deeper than simply learning to cook and clean, a shift far beyond Don's ability to teach. I struggled on my own to adapt to Relief Society culture, catch up on Church doctrine, visit teach, learn Primary songs, and figure out how to cook from food storage.

I kept trying, despite my feelings of inadequacy. The voice proved to be right. Now two years into the adventure, my marriage is again stable and happy. Our family has been sealed in the temple. We have two daughters, with a third on the way. We have acquired a year's supply of food and planted a garden. I have learned to organize closets, grind wheat, and sprout beans. Don and I are both serving in leadership positions in our ward.

Most of the time I am pleased with this new life. But as my practical mothering abilities have grown, my aspirations have become increasingly spiritual. Instead of worrying about the state of my house, I worry about the state of my soul. Am I being patient enough? Kind enough? Loving enough? Despite my progress in meeting the external benchmarks I set for myself, a long distance still stretches between my present (albeit much improved) self and the ideal mother who lives in my imagination.

Today is a perfect example. After a night of little sleep

and a day of active children, I lost my temper and spoke harshly. I retreated to my bedroom for a spiritual pick-me-up with Church history, but I now find myself more discouraged than when I began.

I eye myself critically in the bathroom mirror. I look like a woman, but reading a description of Mary Fielding Smith is enough to make me doubt it. She crossed the plains as a grieving widow, with small children in tow and little of the support she should have been granted by her fellow Saints. All I have to do is teach co-op preschool once a week and fix dinner in my modern kitchen. She apparently fulfilled her responsibilities with enough love to inspire adoration and future faithfulness in her children. I can't seem to make it through an ordinary day without losing my temper.

Some mother. Some woman.

My thoughts drift to possible remedies for my situation. Attend the temple more? Read more scriptures? Fast longer? Pray harder? Already pushed nearly to my own breaking point, I feel rising frustration at the seeming impossibility of it all. The many demands on my time seem to prevent me from doing anything more to improve myself.

Desperate, I fall to my knees. "Heavenly Father," I pray, "I'm sorry. I try so hard, but I feel so inadequate. I want to be better. I want to be an angel mother too, but right now I don't even know how I'm going to make it through the rest of today."

My focus is interrupted by the cheerful voice of my four-year-old daughter. "Guess what, Mommy?" she chirps. "I made you a present."

I look up and try to smile. "Thanks, honey."

She proudly holds up a pink, plastic headband with a ring of paper taped to the top, like a halo.

"What is it?" I ask, slow to accept what my eyes and heart are telling me.

"It's a hat for you. I made it because you're my angel mother."

Expectations

Kristen Ridge

Dear Shaelynn,

You're almost one year old as I write this letter. It amazes me to realize that by the time I give this to you, you will be a grown woman—perhaps a wife, perhaps even an expectant mother!

Expectations. I had so many of those before you were born. I like to prepare for everything, big or small. I like to make the best out of any situation. I love to organize my life in such a way that things go nice and smooth, so I can focus my energy on enjoying an experience rather than stressing out about it.

During the months that I was pregnant with you, I read and read about pregnancy, delivery, and motherhood. Your dad told me I should read a bit less—he thought that I would get crazy ideas in my head, which I sometimes did. But mostly, he wanted me to read less because he knew that I might set myself up for disaster if I thought I could control each and every thing that happened to me or you. I kept reading; it was so much fun to read about your developing body, about the changes happening in mine, and about what I would need to do to take care of you as an infant.

One of the things that meant the most to me as a mother-to-be was breastfeeding. To me, that was the mark of a conscientious, unselfish, and intelligent mother. I naturally read a lot about the topic, focusing my efforts on *The Womanly Art of Breastfeeding*. I read it all before you were born. I had worked for Early Head Start for a year, and had taught women about breastfeeding. I thought I knew pretty much everything there was to know about it.

And then you were born.

I nursed you right there in the delivery room. You had an extremely strong suck. It really shocked me how strong your jaws were, and how even being so very tiny and delicate, you had such strength. It really hurt me, and I wondered if you were latching on properly. But the nurses told me that you were, so even though I gritted my teeth as you ate, I trusted them and continued on. Through that night, I nursed several more times, each time with more pain. By morning, and at the end of your first day of life, my nipples were all torn up.

This wasn't what I had pictured. I had imagined a little soreness, a little tenderness. Pain, maybe. But not *unbearable* pain. Surely by the next day it would go a lot better.

But things didn't improve. At home, you woke up hungry every two hours, sometimes even more often. I wanted to look forward to it, but instead felt sick every time you cried with an empty stomach. I applied the lanolin that the nurses had sent home with me. I tried so hard to change your suck to something that wasn't so painful, but your little jaws were clenched so tight I couldn't do a thing. I broke the suction over and over again, then grabbed my books and held the pages open with one hand to examine the latch-on illustrations.

Cradle hold. Cross-cradle hold. Football hold. I peered at the baby's mouth in the picture, then stared at yours. I bit my lip, swallowed five or six times, and pushed your mouth near me to help you try—over and over we tried. Time after time, I broke the suction.

"Perry," I finally cried out to your father. "I can't nurse any more if it keeps hurting like this, not one more time."

But as scared as I was to keep nursing, I was even more terrified of stopping. Breastfeeding symbolized all of my hopes for you to be a healthy baby, and for me to be a good mother. Your health, your growth—your survival. It was all up to me. Nursing was supposed to be the epitome of womanhood, like *The Womanly Art of Breastfeeding* had implied.

"Womanly" implies grace, loveliness, poise, pleasure. Instead, I felt miserable and wretched.

I took you to a pediatrician for your three-week checkup. You were only six ounces heavier than at birth. My heart raced, my throat felt swollen, and phrases such as "underweight," and "Is she nursing okay?" hovered around my head.

I felt ill, overwhelmed, and angry all at once. We'd just moved and were living out of suitcases. In the midst of packing up the apartment, I'd been nursing every two hours. Yes, it had still been painful, but you had been eating—hadn't you? I had heard you suck, watched your ear lobes twitch just like the books said, watched your jaws move . . .

I forced myself not to cry. The doctor kindly wondered aloud if perhaps my body had not produced enough milk because of the stress of the move. Could that be it? She recommended that we go to a wonderful doctor specializing in feeding issues.

This specialist spent two hours with us during our first visit. She weighed you, naked, then had me feed you on one side. After you ate, she weighed you again, calculating the grams you had gained in liquid measurement. In twenty minutes you had swallowed only half an ounce of milk.

I felt myself die inside. *She must be mistaken,* I thought.

"Let's do the right side now," I said. "I have a lot more milk on that one." I did. Back onto the scale. You'd drunk a sixth of an ounce.

I felt like an idiot. Here I had been bragging to everyone for the past few weeks that my body was making extra milk. It was so great that I wasn't having any problems making enough. Putting the pieces together, I realized what had really been happening. You weren't *getting* the milk . . . that's why I had so much.

Embarrassed, I wondered how I didn't notice something as profound as whether you were actually eating. I still protested, thinking this *couldn't* be what was happening. "But look at how she's sucking," I said, pointing. "See how her jaw is moving? It looks right to me."

"Yes, she is sucking," the doctor said. "But she's not *swallowing*. Here . . . let me help you listen and distinguish between the two sounds."

I bent my head forward to listen for your swallow, my mind was blank, numb. I felt utterly beside myself in confusion and sadness. I listened, and there—you made a soft gulping noise. The swallows were few and far between, but I heard them.

But all along, you hadn't been swallowing more than a few times each minute. Again, a flood of failure dumped over my head, drenching my whole body and heart with feelings of inadequacy and desperation. I had been living in an illusion, literally. What I'd thought was happening was actually the opposite of reality. You had been so hungry, for so long.

And it was because of me.

We got back into the car. I was supposed to be driving, but I just sat in the driver's seat, motionless. I couldn't move my hand to put the key in. I just stared. Dad tried to get me to say something, but nothing was there. I felt dead. After about twenty minutes, Dad tried talking to me.

"I've never felt so empty and sad," I said when I finally spoke. "I don't feel like doing anything. I just want to die."

His response was, "Kristen, you're depressed. We're going to go home and get some help for you."

Help? I didn't even know what I needed.

I was a failure for unknowingly underfeeding you all that time. Here I had been giving 200 percent to you, and it hadn't been enough. That's what hurt the most—the feeling that I wasn't capable of meeting your basic needs. I had failed in something that was a given: keeping you alive, giving you the nourishment you needed. If I couldn't even *feed* you properly, how would I ever manage other parenting issues?

I imagined myself as a grandmother having conversations with other women as we sat in rocking chairs and looked back on life.

Friend: "My daughter chose to do drugs at age thirty, even after we raised her right. It's too bad she decided to take that path."

Me: "I starved my baby girl as an infant and didn't even know it until she was a month old. Everything else just fell apart after that. I guess I wasn't cut out for motherhood."

I see now how ridiculous and irrational my thoughts

were at the time. But back then I was scared, so scared. Scared enough to try one more time.

After that terrible trip to the doctor's office, I took some time to rest. I was physically and emotionally worn out from the delivery, the move, and now this. Everything had piled up.

After a nap, I could think logically again. The specialist had said you'd need to be supplemented with formula while my milk supply was developing and you were learning how to nurse correctly.

She had encouraged me, saying, "The most important thing isn't that you are exclusively breastfeeding, but that your daughter begins to gain weight and is healthy." I slowly began to realize that she was right. You would be able to be nourished with formula. And I would still be a good mother. Possibly even a wonderful one.

Throughout the rest of that afternoon, I felt more energetic than I'd felt in days. I felt a lightness in my body. Whether it was the Spirit comforting me and giving me a boost of confidence, or simply the relief that came from a huge paradigm shift triggered by this wonderful specialist, that afternoon marked the beginning of a big change.

You and I started over. A small well of hope grew each time I fed you and throughout each nap you took when I got to rest and rejuvenate myself. A new set of skills to practice gave me a challenge to look forward to as well. Each time you were hungry, I gathered my pillows, set them up around my back, and put several under you. I waited for your little mouth to lunge toward me, and as you latched on, I used my forefinger to push your bottom jaw down as far as I could, so that you would open wider.

After several days of doing this a dozen times a day, I heard the soft sounds of swallows more often. Such a wonderful sound; it was a sign of success for both of us—you were learning to eat, and my body was making more milk.

Every few days, I took you in to be weighed. You were such a little champion—you did so well at gaining weight, usually several ounces a week. There was one day that I will always remember more than the others: September 1, 2006. You were about six weeks old. A week had gone by since your last weight check. This time you gained thirteen ounces in seven days. The doctor was amazed; she said she'd never seen a comeback quite like yours.

After about four weeks, we'd done it, together. You gained weight, my body healed, and we became a great team. And we kept moving forward.

You're now about to complete your first year of life. As I see your independence grow daily, as you boldly tumble and scoot and do gymnastics across the house, my mind swirls with thoughts of the future and the person you will become. I want to meet all your needs as you grow. I hope you will trust me enough to tell me what you need so I can help you.

But my expectations for myself as a mother have changed. Before you were born, I thought that if I worked hard enough, I'd be able to do everything right. Now I realize that I probably won't always recognize exactly what you need, and exactly when you need it.

It's better this way. The pain and challenges you experience will be chances for you to develop strength, and to look inside yourself for the answers.

You and I will experience many challenges as you grow, and you can count on a number of them being caused by my mistakes. But when those times come, I'll remember the only thing that matters—that we keep trying.

I'll look back on the hundreds of times I nursed you. Your rosy cheeks, long eyelashes, and your hand gripping my thumb. You looking up at me, smiling at me. The sound of you swallowing.

I'll see your eyes getting heavy, your body melting into my arms. I'll feel the sweetness that came from fighting to give you what I knew was the best thing for you, and the happiness of finally succeeding.

And I'll remember that we have sweet ties holding us together: bonds of trust, perseverance, and love.

Given and Giver

Darlene Young

Mother-fluids:
Tears and milk and sweat.
Filling and draining, at once,
I thirst.

Hurtling through the day,
Or else meandering.
(Both perilous, both right.)

Haunted and hungry,
Yet blossoming, widening,
I abound as I yearn.

A whole universe
To some, and still
Less than the dust.

Bent forward, I fret,
Bent back to regret.
Waver and wash to and fro.

Careen, sometimes,
With joy or fear,
But still it is a dance.

Ebb and flow,
Enfold and reach,
Wait and watch,
Weep and sing.

They Weren't Mine to Keep

Melonie Cannon

They weren't mine to keep, nor mine to give away, but when the two children were taken out of my arms and into the waiting embrace of their new mothers, I felt my heart expand, making new space for joy and astonishing tenderness. For twenty-four hours I was their mother. That was twenty-one years ago.

I was seventeen years old when I arrived in the capital city of San Salvador the summer between my junior and senior years of high school. I would spend the summer with an old friend's family in that humid country in Central America. Up to that point, my life had revolved around schoolwork and boys, not necessarily in that order. I looked forward to a change.

Although I learned many lessons and faced many challenges during my stay, I never expected to learn anything about children, love, or motherhood. In hindsight, it's obvious that God had other plans when He plunked me down in the labyrinth of wide, tree-lined boulevards and filthy alleys that is San Salvador.

It was a city of contrasts—stucco mansions with gated entries stood within walking distance of tin-roofed shacks.

Chauffeurs drove teenage socialites to fancy restaurants while lean, mongrel dogs shared food with the poor in the streets. Grim-faced men holding machine guns stood on the corners of the main thoroughfares, while housewives with groceries walked by laughing and talking as though the threat of hostility was as common as a thank-you. Convoys of soldiers passed us on the road as we dined on a lobster picnic in the country.

For me, the contrasts ran deeper than appearances. I felt an undercurrent of violence and deception as strong as the tremors that sometimes shook my bed. The soul of the country was torn in half by civil war. Stories were rampant of guerrillas kidnapping people and taking them to the mountains to join their forces. Many women were raped, and the resulting undesired offspring were left in dumpsters or orphanages.

I cannot describe the shock it was for a Utah girl who grew up in a Mormon home to see another world for the first time. When the rain came down in torrents, I put on my swimming suit and stood under the warm deluge, letting myself cry as much as the San Salvadorian sky.

I missed home. I missed being innocent. I missed walking through life with my eyes shut. Once I visited a mental institution where patients scuttled about naked in a huge dirt courtyard, moaning from hunger and loss of mind. Some were tied to beds and screaming. Even in my friend's own house I witnessed abuse, deception, and raging social inequality. At the time, the social environment in San Salvador was as suffocating as the humidity.

One of the great reprieves that summer was visiting an orphanage every week. Though the children lived in squalor, they were so happy. The children had one soccer ball, which they prized as though it were made of gold. They smiled easily as they kicked it around the dirt floors and laughed. Even the babies, tied to highchairs, were patient as they waited for someone to feed them. The conditions of the place made my heart ache, so it was a relief to see a little bit of happiness. I wished I could take all of the children home.

Toward the end of the summer, the opportunity arose for me to be a carrier for an adoption agency and bring two babies to waiting families in Utah. I considered the chance a gift from God.

The agency director brought the two children, a boy and a girl, on the morning of my departure. One was eleven-month-old Alejandra, and the other, nine-month-old Ernesto. He had fat legs and a ready smile beneath a disheveled bush of black hair. He could sit up and reach for toys. Although he had some rashes, he seemed quite healthy.

Alejandra did not. She was very small for her age and had cigarette burns up and down her legs. Her hair was stringy and dark. At first she was withdrawn, but after a few minutes, she clung to me like a little monkey. I had never been held like that before, and it stirred a feeling deep inside that I did not recognize.

I was needed.

I had no idea how difficult the next twenty-four hours would be. At the time, my task seemed straightforward enough—get on a plane with the kids, stop at the Los Angeles airport for a couple of hours, then go home to Salt Lake City through Phoenix, arriving late in the evening to meet the expecting parents. I was given a diaper bag with baby food and two large envelopes with explicit instructions not to lose them. Inside were the children's plane tickets and the adoption papers needed to get into the United States.

I loaded the diaper bags, documents, and my luggage into the family car for the hour-long drive to the airport. I held the babies tight on my lap as we wove through the city streets. I was going home! All would be well for me again, and my two little charges would have a new life! Every moment of the drive to the long airport lines seemed to last forever. Once our large bags were checked, the family I had stayed with all summer kissed me goodbye at a security checkpoint and left. Alone now, I suddenly felt very afraid, but with determination I slung my bags over my shoulder and lifted the two babies into my arms. I had no car seat or stroller. Just me—or so I thought.

After going through security, my first hurdle arrived: a tax I knew nothing about. A worker told me that I couldn't leave the country without paying what amounted to about fifty dollars. I didn't know whether I was being swindled, but it didn't matter; I had only ten dollars left.

I had been working since I was fifteen to scrape together enough money for this trip. The summer had drained my wallet. I wandered aimlessly through the airport, not knowing what to do. I couldn't reach my host by telephone before my flight left. Calling my family in America was futile—what could they do from there? I didn't have enough money to change our tickets to the next day, and my Spanish wasn't good enough to argue with the airport employees.

It had been only twenty minutes since I was dropped off, and I was utterly alone, scared, and penniless. I prayed as I walked, the children getting heavier with each step.

As I entered a large waiting area, I looked for a place to put the children down so I could think and pray harder. A tall, gray-haired man moved in front of me and asked in accented English, "Do you need any help?"

I frantically explained my predicament. He reached in his pocket, handed me the correct amount, smiled, and walked away. I thanked him and thanked him, but he never even turned around.

While waiting for our flight, I tucked the adoption envelopes into the front pocket of my carry-on. An airline employee asked if I needed help boarding. Gratefully, I said yes. He followed me with my carry-on bags while I carried the children. I settled into a two-seated row near the front of the airplane. The employee put my suitcase above me. Ernesto was on my lap and Alejandra sat next to me, seat-belted and scared, looking as tiny as a raisin in a field of fat grapes. A stewardess closed the overhead bins, and made the announcements. The attendants checked our seatbelts. I leaned back in my seat, grateful to be heading home. A worker closed the airplane door, and suddenly, a jolt went through me. Something wasn't right.

I stood, holding Ernesto on one hip, and opened the overhead bin. I checked for the brown envelopes in the front pocket of my bag. They were not there. I started waving and yelling at the stewardess. "Stop the plane! Don't leave!" She ran down the aisle, and I handed her Ernesto. "Watch the kids!"

I ran to the closed door and made them open it up. Unbelievably, they did, no questions asked. Where could the envelopes be? I had sat in the same seat in the waiting area the entire time. I ran down the long hallway to the seating area. It was deserted. But there, resting on my seat, were two large, brown envelopes. Shuddering with relief, I scooped them up and hurried back to the plane. It was clear to me that despite the opposition I faced, the way was opening for these children to get to the United States.

I finally settled in for the long flight, or so I'd hoped. I soon discovered that there was a rhythm to caring for children. The hours on the airplane were my first introduction to the beat. Crying, feedings, diaper changes, whispered songs, rocking, and finger games were all new to me, but I learned quickly as I cared for two completely powerless infants.

I studied their little fingernails and the details of their eyelashes. Their breath felt like warm mist against my neck. For the moment, I was all they had in the world. A great tenderness and a new consciousness came over me. *Is this what it feels like to be a mother?* I thought. *To never have one moment to think about yourself, to be so wrapped up in another's needs that nothing else seems to matter?*

By the time we landed, I was exhausted but bowled over by love. I waited until the last passenger got off the plane, then gathered our belongings that had been scattered across two seats. As I looked back at the empty seats, I felt a great sense of accomplishment. Surely the hardest part was over.

Landing in the Los Angeles airport is like landing in a

small city. I didn't have a map or directions, but I knew I had to find the place called "customs." By the time I walked into the hallway of the international terminal, only a few stragglers remained. They were far away, walking at a clipped pace toward a mutual goal. There were no airline employees to guide my way or any baggage carts. I walked for a while before finding a room where my luggage stood by itself. Where were all the people?

I found one weary worker, who pointed toward a giant empty hallway. "Customs," he said.

The next half hour felt like an eternity. I couldn't carry the children and pull the luggage at the same time, so I would trade off, carrying and pulling in increments. I walked with the children about twenty feet before setting them on the floor. Then I went back for the luggage and pulled it to where they sat waiting. On and on I went, my arms getting more and more tired with each trip. The entire time I never saw a soul in that hallway. The "city" was empty.

I dragged the luggage one last time to where the babies sat, knowing I couldn't heave the luggage or carry the children another step. I knelt on the floor with them, crying, a heap of helplessness. Again, I turned to the only recourse I had—God.

Heavenly Father, I prayed, *I cannot pick these babies up again. I have gone as far as I can go. Please send someone to help me. I have another plane to catch, and I cannot make it without help.* The instant I finished, a door opened, and out walked two men dressed as airline employees.

"What are you doing here?" one asked. Stunned to see another human being, I didn't answer for a moment.

"Do you need some help?" asked the other.

The floodgates of words and tears opened, and I explained my problem. Each of the men picked up a baby and a piece of luggage. I carried the other bags, and we marched, like a vagabond band of army stragglers, toward customs. Something great had happened. God had answered my prayer immediately. He knew my needs and He knew these children. I would never be the same again.

The men walked us right past the long lines at customs and into a small office. There, the children got their pictures taken and all the paperwork finished. I stood by and watched, grateful and humbled by their help.

When we went to board the connecting flight from Los Angeles to Phoenix, we couldn't get on. The children's tickets were for a different airline from mine, with a similar sounding name. For a brief, irrational moment, an alarm flashed through me: I'd be separated from my children.

They weren't my children, of course, nor would I be separated from them, but I couldn't control the overwhelming feeling of panic. Everything on the journey that could go wrong had, but I was learning to rely on the Lord with each new challenge.

My kind cousin, who'd met us on the other side of customs, loaded up the luggage and took us to his home outside L.A., where we spent a short night before returning to the airport. Showing great generosity, my cousin bought a ticket for me on the same airline as the children.

The two-hour flight was bittersweet for me. I held both babies in my lap and rubbed my chin against their dark heads. I imagined their future in America and what their lives might bring. I prayed over them, hoping that their new families would love them deeply. Because of all the opposition they'd already had in their young lives, I felt they had great missions to perform—Alejandra, shy and small, but fearless, and Ernesto, stout and sturdy, cuddly and curious. The charm they held for me at our meeting only twenty-four hours before had turned into a deep love.

When the plane landed, I loaded up our things and eagerly picked up the children for my final walk down the airline ramp. This was the end of our journey together. This was the moment that would change their lives forever—the moment their new mothers would first hold them. I felt apprehensive, almost unwilling to let them go.

My own mother met me right outside the airline door, her arms outstretched to help carry one of the children. My time with them was very brief, just a day in thousands of days to come, but my emotions were intense.

"No. I brought them this far," I told her. "I'll take them the rest of the way. They're mine now. Mine to give away."

There is a photo of me after I had given Ernesto to his new family and turned to Alejandra's. Her thin, brown arms are wrapped around my neck. She seems confused. She clings to me. Showing above her tiny head, my large eyes are pained and weary. We are reluctant to let go of one another.

No words can describe the emotions when I stretched out my arms to give these children to their new mothers. The pure joy on the faces of those women is sealed in my memory. I was so happy for the children, but I knew that I'd probably never see them again.

In twenty-four hours, Alejandra and her traveling brother had taught me more about motherhood than years of babysitting had. I felt, for the first time, what it was like to have someone totally rely on me for everything. At the same time, I had learned to totally rely on my Father in Heaven.

Like an empty pail thrown into a deep well, I was filled with awe at the give-and-take of that eternal partnership. Who would've thought that two tiny babies who passed through my life for only one day could initiate me into the marvelous world of motherhood?

It's been twenty-one years since I saw Ernesto and Alejandra. After all these years, I still think about them. I have four children of my own now. But the lessons those two sweet babies taught me have remained with me.

The first time I held my son, I again felt that same utter helplessness. He relied solely on me. I felt overwhelmed by what was required of me, unsure how to proceed. Each child that has come into my life since has clung to me with total trust, just like Ernesto and Alejandra did. Strangers to each other, we were flung together like oil and water and expected to thrive.

After the birth of each of my children, I've asked myself, "How can I make it? How can I get through this?" But my past experiences give me reassurance that if I turn to the Lord, all will come about as it is supposed to be.

Even when I am so bone-tired I can barely move my body to lift that last child into bed, change another diaper, fix another meal, or hug the sobs away, I think of moments like the one in the giant airport hallway when I had collapsed on the floor, unable to go another step. Then I pray to the Lord to give me one more minute of energy or patience. He does. On days when I think I cannot make it one more minute, He has sent a person willing to give an extra set of hands, just like the airline workers did. Sometimes that person is one of my own children, who leans into me and gives me an unexpected and affectionate hug, coupled with a "thanks" or "I love you, Mom." These are the moments of joy.

Motherhood also brings moments of fear and panic, much like when I learned Ernesto and Alejandra weren't booked on the same flight as mine. I get the same feeling now when one of my children is out of sight in a public space. I might lose them for just a few seconds, but the overwhelming panic that floods my heart and limbs during those moments is the same feeling I had so long ago.

You cannot think with any sense when your child might be missing or terribly hurt. An electrical current jolts its way to your heart and imagination. The earth seems to open up underneath your running feet. There is the sensation of falling but never landing. Those are the motherhood moments when prayers fall freely like water from a loosed faucet. You turn everything over to God's waiting and willing hands.

I imagine our Father in Heaven trusts us to be willing to accept motherhood on all its demanding terms as he sends His spirits down to our waiting hands. I can imagine the pain of parting and the hope He has that we'll love His children as much as He does.

When I handed Alejandra and Ernesto over to their new mothers, I knew the children would not remember me. I hoped their new parents would perhaps tell them about the journey we made together. Maybe, when the children felt down, a faint memory of being loved would rise inside and they would know that someone distant dreamed of their future and its amazing possibilities. This is surely how God feels about us. He wants us to think of Him and know we are loved. He alone knows the full possibilities of our lives.

Because of His great wisdom, He sent me to San Salvador when I was just seventeen to learn about motherhood and its indelible relationship with God. Because of His great generosity, I have four little children of my own to magnify this lesson and solidify my relationship with the Divine. Because of His great love, Alejandra and Ernesto touched my life.

In a sense, I was their "mother" for only twenty-four hours, but what I learned from them is forever mine to keep.

The Yoke of Wisdom

Melissa Young

A hot July sun warms my back as I stand on the thresh-old of our new home. It's a perfect day for moving. Our old life lies one hundred miles to the north, left behind for a promising new job and the chance to attend graduate school. I survey the piles of our life cluttering the floor, the stacks of sacks and boxes, the weedy yard outside. I drop my gaze and breathe deeply, then smile.

A new beginning.

Three weeks later, my hands grip the cold tile counter-top as I watch a faint line appear in a tiny plastic window. I am pregnant! Excitement ignites my entire body, flushing my cheeks and quickening my pulse. I literally dance for joy. My little toddler's eyes widen in wonder at my unusual exit from the bathroom. I am five weeks along. Everything is already there; it only needs time to grow. I place a hand on my stom-ach, in wonder at the mystery of this person. Singing my way down the hall, I begin to think of new ways to arrange the bedroom furniture.

I spend the next few weeks unpacking boxes, trying to get as much done as possible. Morning sickness has yet to make its queasy appearance, and I secretly hope I won't get sick this time. Perhaps if I'm not sick, it means I'm carrying a girl! I fold maternity clothes and imagine; my heart soars.

A new hope.

Days later, I grip the bathroom countertop again and feel a prickle of fear at a smear of blood. Staring at the dark stain, my thoughts begin to race. My mother bled during her pregnancies; her babies were all fine. I run to the next room and pull my pregnancy reference book from the shelf. The pages shake in my hands as I read every entry on miscarriage. Worry clutches my stomach.

I call my mom, asking about her experiences again. She gives comfort but doesn't have answers. "Call a doctor," she advises. I need to find one first.

The next day is my brother's wedding. I wander the temple grounds, drawing strength from the feel of my husband's hand encircling mine. Looking at the granite spires, I try to think of family and eternity, but my body will not let me forget the blood still issuing from it. In a quiet moment, I speak to my sister-in-law, who recently lost one of the twin embryos she was carrying. Her reassuring words do not mask the concern in her eyes.

That evening, we prepare for the reception. The cramps and bleeding have worsened, making it difficult to stand. I put on my long, black-and-white formal gown. I smile for the pictures. I join the line and greet wedding guests. I accept the congratulations of family friends who are thrilled to hear of our coming addition. I fight the tightness in my throat and the stinging in my eyes.

My brother and his new wife wonder why I leave the line so often.

Earlier in the evening, the bride gave gifts to all of the bridesmaids: a necklace with an empty pendant and an oyster containing a pearl to be placed inside the pendant. The color of each pearl has symbolic meaning. From a secluded corner, I watch the girls erupt into squeals and giggles as each one opens her shell. One finds lavender for love; others find peach for health, gold for wealth, cream for success. Desperate for a sign, I stare at the rough oyster in my hand and will it to hold a peach pearl—peach for the health of the new life struggling inside me. I crack the oyster . . . a white pearl falls to my lap. I exhale.

White, for wisdom.

After placing the pearl in the pendant, I slip the cool silver strand around my neck and feel the yoke of wisdom settle like a weight. The sign has been given.

A new heaviness.

The next morning, I lie on a hard table in a sterile room. The doctor I met five minutes ago slides the ultrasound sensor over the cold gel on my belly. His silence is unnerving. I stare at the fuzzy image on the monitor, searching for a flicker of heartbeat.

"There's no baby," he finally says. "I don't think there ever was a real baby. There is some tissue here, but it has mostly disintegrated." He briefly explains the procedure performed in such cases and asks when I would like to have it done. I shake my head, unable to think. Everything I've focused on for six weeks is not only gone, it never existed. My hopes are dust and ashes. I want to go home with my husband and finish this in the privacy of our home. The doctor seems an unwelcome intrusion.

Hours later, the cramping becomes more rhythmic. An icy thought chills me as I recognize the waves of pain: I am in labor. It feels different because my uterus is so small this time. Suddenly terrified of what I'll deliver and how I'll dispose of it, I call the doctor's office. They instruct me to go to the hospital.

In the labor and delivery room, I hear the sounds of other women and their families. Though the curtain shields my view, I can still hear the bustling, happy noises. I turn my face to the wall, the joyful voices present at my son's birth echoing through my memory. I wonder now if grief darkened any of the rooms that surrounded my joy. Hollow emptiness magnifies my past insensitivity. But I could not have known sorrow then, not when all was happy innocence. Grief now expands my awareness, but the bite of knowledge has bit-tered my tongue. I wonder at Eve's ability to have chosen this fruit.

One week later, a good friend from our old neighbor-hood calls. I try to sound normal—the way I've tried to sound with all of the smiling strangers around me. She is not fooled. The tears I've fought every day spill over as I tell her about our loss. We cry together, and I feel a little less far away from the support of friends.

"I'm so sorry. I should have called sooner," she says, telling me about an impression she had received to call sev-eral days ago. This catches me off guard; I am amazed, both at her spiritual sensitivity and at God's awareness of me.

A new awe.

One year later, my feelings are still tender but less raw. A friend and I are enjoying a neighborly living room chat when she expresses her confusion at the grief of another woman who recently miscarried.

"There was never even a baby," she says. "How can she grieve over nothing?"

She's unaware of my experience, so I'm unsure how to answer. A baby is a powerful, unseen force for an expectant woman, even when it's intangible to others. I knew I hadn't lost a real child, but the line on the pregnancy test was real. My dreams were real; my love was real. I grieved for my child-to-be, for everything that could have been and then wasn't. I felt the sting of injustice, knowing that my memory would serve as the only reality for this potential child—a child everyone else would forget. And even though it seemed foolish, I grieved for the loss of my innocent, youthful ignorance of suffering. The peace of inexperience would never return.

Yet with that loss came new perspective. I look at faces around me differently now. I wonder what sorrows lie behind the smiles. Occasionally the heavy weight is evidenced—a tear, an aching whisper of story. But bearing that weight creates strength—a greater ability to bear the mortal yoke.

I look at my newborn son sleeping on a blanket next to us. Beauty for ashes. I think of how every common twinge during his pregnancy brought a stab of fear. Gratitude for his safe arrival filled me more than would have been possible before my loss. Bitter magnified the sweet.

I think of my white pearl and Eve's fruit—the wrenching sacrifice of innocence for wisdom. *Yes,* I think to myself. *It is better to pass through, that we may know.* Then with our knowing and our strength, we praise Him who makes our burdens light.

My friend's puzzled question still hangs in the air. I quietly share my story.

A new strength.

Old truth.

Encircling

Kylie Turley

Miscarried late one night when I was groggy
Perhaps a skinny, laughing girl,
With soft blonde hair and green eyes
As I dreamed the night before.
My almost-baby was gone before I understood
The cramping pains that buckled my knees
And sent me whimpering to the bathroom.
I would have called out for help or comfort
If I weren't embarrassed
Unsure about this intimacy. So physical
This process. My body shared, then not.

In my mind, I call her Eden, a name
Without a mother or a child.
Still, I miss
Her head tucked into my neck, breathing softly,
Her warm-sleep body gathered in my arms—
Even after holding other children of my creation.
Like Eve, I suppose.

On a brisk December birthday
I would have swaddled

Her in a blanket or two to take her home.
Instead, an early birth-death: May,
So bright and shiny. Two days later
I sat in the sun by the pool—
Swimming suit taut over my empty stomach.
Every year now there's that circling,
The May, the December, the May.
She's a thought—brief—
I find myself thinking another without realizing
But the return
Is a comfort, a marking, a naming
Of Eden,
Mother of my mothering.

Small Sacrifice

Lani B. Whitney

Creation. Creation of little people. Little bodies being formed in the womb. We mammals are interesting creatures; our motherhood astounds me. I'm confused during my early pregnancy as I make the very enlightened discovery that every person I see had to be born to get here. Born? Yes, every human being on earth was inside a mother's womb and eventually came out into the light. All those people in the grocery store, in the parking lot, all those school children—all of them, born!

During the first few months of pregnancy I'm amazed at what women go through. The nonstop nausea that permeates every second of my days in the first three months always begins with the same routine. First, I am strong. I am just barely pregnant, and I feel great. I've gotten in shape physically and mentally. This time, nothing is going to get me down. I am older now, wiser, and just have things in better control. I am in control—me, alone. You'd think I was my own savior—with my organizing and hard-working attitude being what keeps this family running.

Everything is in order; our home seems to be running pretty efficiently. My husband and I have prayed about another baby, and we feel good about it. We're excited to share the news of another member of our family with our children. I await the nausea, but it doesn't come. I am, after all, three whole weeks pregnant. The lack of sickness makes me nervous. Am I really pregnant? But, yes, the test was positive, and there are other signs. I overconfidently begin to think this time will be different from the last.

"I just didn't eat healthy enough back then," I say to my family. "This time I'm just not sick—isn't it great?"

Then, sure enough, three or four days later it begins—the nonstop monster of queasiness. It's hard to open my eyes; it's hard to *close* my eyes. My feet and hands are cold. I feel like I'm trapped in my body. No food sounds appealing. The colors around me are too bright, too ugly. The scent of my husband's deodorant suddenly repulses me. My children's breath is equally bad. The sky is too low and too dark. When will I learn? This is the fifth pregnancy I've had during the winter holidays. Suddenly, almost instantly, my jeans are uncomfortable at the waist.

"I will not let this get me," I say over and over. "I am in control." I beg in my prayers for some relief. Then, when it does come, a few minutes here or there, I fear that something must be wrong.

I vow to my husband and friends that this will be the last pregnancy for me. I cannot do it again—*ever.* I write this down in my journal for future reference. I must remember how difficult the experience is—how torturous it is. Isn't it strange how this overconfident woman who was in control of all is suddenly a helpless child, wondering how and if she will make it through this day, this hour, this minute? I don't have a choice; I must go through it.

As I begin to ponder pain and suffering, I look up all the scriptures I can under these topics, searching to make sense of it. Trying to put my short-term misery in perspective, I think of others who are sick—really sick—for the long term. I think of people who suffer more than I can imagine—children in hospitals with diseases in small pale bodies. I think about the Lord's pain and suffering, of God's suffering as He watches us.

I wonder how and why we must suffer. I am level with the ground. I am thankful for even the smallest kindness, getting choked up when mere acquaintances routinely ask me how I am. As I awake in the morning, I lie still, fighting off the moment when I can no longer make the baby wait in her crib. I have to get up. We head to the kitchen for breakfast.

It's amazing how quickly our diet has gone from health-conscious to instant, preserved, and full of refined sugar. If it's frozen, we have it. If it's canned, we eat it. I give myself kudos for getting something—anything—on the table, even if it doesn't have enough nutrition to support an ant. I am really accomplishing something if I can take a bath or comb my hair. The questions begin to come as our lives are falling down around us.

"Why do we have children anyway?" And, "This is the plan of . . . happiness?!"

Just when it seems it can't get much worse, something unusual happens: I'm not nauseated for two hours one afternoon. Is something wrong? Gradually, I feel relief for longer and longer periods. I'm almost over it. I mark the calendar days off in black marker. The first trimester is almost over, and relief is coming.

In another week or two I'm on my feet again, already forgetting the seemingly endless misery of the last few months. I'm a humbler, better version of me than the self-sufficient woman of twelve weeks ago. Knowing who my Savior is, I have a refreshed memory of my reliance on Him. I have begged for His grace and help in my affliction, and my soul has a tangible sympathy for others who are suffering. Will I go through this again? Yes! I hope so. Already I can imagine a small head covered in dark hair—the newness of creation arriving in our family. My small sacrifice is worth it to meet this little soul. And now my prayers will not be for relief, but to please let this little one stay for a long, long time.

Ultrasound

Emily Milner

Expose my belly: swollen,
white, marked with winding lines.
Within: a bumping child,
bound and fed by blood
and waters, liquid prison,
tissue home. I watch his blurry,
pulsing heart, see the shape
of arms and hips, the thin
clenched hands, the wound-up cord.
We both await release: the pain
and freedom of an empty womb.
His freedom binds me more,
a bond I chose, one I embraced
with gentle fear. We both
will cry when we're set free.
We both must learn to breathe.

Finding Myself on Google

Emily Milner

There are three references to me on Google. The first is on page six. Before that I wade through pages of references to not-me Emily Milners: genealogy charts, a talented high school violinist, a devout Catholic from Georgia, a fourth-year physics major. The first two actual references to me are from a forum I haven't posted on in years; the last one comes from my husband, who e-mailed something to a political website last fall using my e-mail address.

It's on page seven.

I've done nothing worthy of mention on Google for years. It doesn't take much to be listed there: a page referencing employees at a business, a brief line in a newspaper article. In spite of the ease of appearing on Google, however, my presence there is almost nonexistent. I've been living a home-centered life, and my yellow, split-level house doesn't register on Google either. Just after high school—if Google had been around back then—you could have looked me up and discovered awards, prizes, scholarships.

That's how I defined myself: by all my public achievements. But even at the top of my academic glory, I knew I'd always feel incomplete without a home and a family. I wanted children, and I wanted to stay home with them. It was a deep need. When I became pregnant with my first child, I felt grateful that God had blessed me with what I most desired.

I don't remember much about the time just after I had Scott. Most of it runs together in a haze, except this conversation with my father. I had gone several days with very little sleep as I tried to nurse my baby, and I was frazzled when I answered the phone.

"How's my grandson?" he said. He sounded too cheerful.

I couldn't handle cheer right then. "I can't do this," I sobbed. "I can't! I can't keep trying to nurse him. I can't go without sleep. I'm a terrible mother! Why am I doing this?"

Dad stayed mostly quiet and let me cry it out. "You'll make it through this," he told me. "You can do it."

But could I? I had thought that giving birth would mean a nice package of "mother skills" somehow appearing when the baby emerged. It didn't turn out that way. I couldn't feed him, couldn't get him to sleep, couldn't even experience that mythical mothering bond that was supposed to make all my sleepless nights worthwhile.

I had to keep going in spite of my awkward mothering. Every day I got a little better at diapering and feeding and entertaining. Eventually I even got a good night's sleep. And I began to have some magical moments. When Scott was seven months old, I sang "Eensy Weensy Spider" to him for the first time. He sat up, still a bit wobbly in his balance, and laughed as I made the hand motions. He'd never laughed like that before. I sang it for him over and over as he laughed and waved his arms.

I wrote about it in my journal, as I wrote down other such mommying moments: little snippets of time that made me feel like a mother, instead of someone just filling in for the real one, who would arrive any minute to take over and return me to my previous life. My journal proved to me that I was making it.

Dad was right. I did it, because I had to. But I was right too: the person I was when I had Scott could not be a mother. I had to change. I gave up part of myself to be a mother, a part I've never seen since. It's the part of me that wrote "A Translation and Commentary of Manuel Cañete's Prologue to the *Obras Completas del Duque de Rivas*" for my Honors thesis. It's the part of me that checked my grades online every so often, just for fun, so I could see the rows of approving A's. It's the part that loved school. Every September I still get nostalgic for new pencils and crisp notebooks. And it is the part that, if I'd done things differently, would be right there on Google.

Scott was almost one when I first heard Sheri Dew's talk on motherhood, "Are We Not All Mothers?" Her words left me discouraged and uplifted at the same time. She said: "In the Lord's language, the word *mother* has layers of meaning. Of all the words they could have chosen to define her role and her essence, both God the Father and Adam called Eve 'the mother of all living' and they did so *before* she ever bore a child. Like Eve, our motherhood began before we were born."[1]

As I listened to these words I wept, from a combination of the Spirit witnessing truth and from my own feelings of inadequacy. If my essential nature was that of a mother, and if sometimes I didn't like being a mother, what did that say about me? I felt like a terrible human being because Eve's mothering heritage was not my natural gift. I had to work at enjoying mothering, give myself mommy pep talks. I missed the Google-able side of myself, sometimes resenting my new job. I worked and prayed and sweated for each new mothering skill. I was not Eve—not even close.

I'm confident Sister Dew didn't intend to make young mothers like me feel inadequate. I think she spoke from the pain and healing of a woman who wanted children but was unable to have them, primarily to women who also experienced her childless grief. In spite of the fact that I had borne a child, I was there too, among the women who were discovering their mothering identity. We were more alike than I realized. I felt humbled to be included in this circle of women; I hadn't experienced their pain, but I needed to learn the same lessons of nurturing. I decided I needed to change. I'd grit my teeth and make myself into the mother I was apparently born to be.

This determination echoed in my heart when Scott turned one. That, to me, was a deadline: I had a year to get used to this baby, and then, as a righteous woman, as someone who wanted a row of celestial A's, it would be time for me to have another baby. This was because, I told myself, it was wrong to use birth control for too long. There were so many spirits waiting to come down that it would be selfish of me to refuse them. Many women couldn't have children at all; I needed to step up to the plate. I might not be naturally good at mothering, but perhaps what I lacked in quality I could make up for in quantity.

That's what I told myself when we started "trying" again.

A few weeks later, Matt was going to put Scott to bed. "Do you want to say goodnight?" he asked.

"I have a terrible headache," I told him. "It's just throbbing. I'm going to say goodnight from here." Scott gave me a hug and kiss and went off to say prayers with Matt. I lay on the couch flipping through channels. My head hurt. I'd never gotten headaches like that before. I expected it to be gone the next day.

But it wasn't. After a few weeks I saw my doctor, got a CAT scan, saw the doctor again. I end up in front of a therapist to try biofeedback for controlling the pain, since other painkillers did not work.

"Before the biofeedback," he said, "I want to talk about what's going on in your life. Is there anything that could be causing the pain? Any stress?"

"Oh, no," I said. "I have a one-year-old, but he's a good baby, and my husband's great. Absolutely no complaints."

"So you're doing well, then?"

"Yes, and we're even . . ." Here, baffling myself, I started to cry. "We're even trying to have another baby, our next one, because we're ready for that."

I didn't realize how *not* ready for another baby I was until I untwisted my convoluted logic in that therapist's chair. I'd read various General Authority quotes concerning birth control that made me feel like it would be sinful to prevent children from coming naturally for very long. I don't know where I got the year limit from; it was just there somehow, maybe since many babies are weaned around that age. After a year's rest, it should be time to have a baby again.

The therapist listened and handed me a box of tissues. "Have you prayed about this?" he asked.

I had, but assumed that God's default answer would be yes. Of course it would be yes. Of course I would need to have another child, and soon. That is what I would need to do to be good, to be righteous, to be a celestial mother. To be Eve.

"God is more merciful than you give Him credit for," he told me. "You're still figuring out how to be a mother. Don't you think God is generous enough to give you more time?"

I left still crying, but bewildered by my tears. I hadn't known such guilt and confusion over having another baby was inside of me. My headache pounded as I thought about the therapist's words and about God's mercy.

The headache didn't go away immediately. I wish I could define the moment when it left. I began to take life more slowly. If I thought of an entire new-baby package together— the nausea, fatigue, and C-section—my headache worsened. But if I thought of creating another Scott, another person, it diminished.

Reading over my journal in those months, I saw "I need to be a better mother" repeated often. But I also saw more and more stories about Scott, about the way he loved to read books—eighteen board books in one sitting—and to type letters with me on the keyboard. The joy I took in his babyhood became more real, less deliberate. I began to believe that it was all right with God for me to enjoy Scott now, to take the time I needed before my next baby. My head cleared, and the pain eased.

The more I appreciated Scott's personality and

sweetness, the more I desired what I wanted to desire: another baby. As I relaxed in my mothering, I began to sense this new spirit. God blessed me with the gift of knowing who Norah was ahead of time, of knowing her name, so that I could prepare my difficult heart to receive her. Even before she was conceived, I thought of her as Norah, not just "another baby." I could feel her presence in our home sometimes; I knew that she wanted to come to our family. Norah would be funny and passionate and strong-willed. She would be excited to play with Scott. Norah, my next child, was real. The more I knew her spirit, the more I was able to think about welcoming her.

A few months after my headaches left, I became pregnant. I knew before the ultrasound that it would be a girl. Norah.

In spite of the peace I had felt over knowing her, I was still scared. I remembered the searing pain of standing up after my C-section, the utter fatigue of those first few sleepless weeks. Could I do this again? The night I went into the hospital, the nurse preparing me for my C-section was surprised to see me crying quietly.

"Are you worried about the surgery?" she asked.

"It's not that," I said. "I'm just scared to have another baby. I don't know if I can do this again. The pain is terrible, you never sleep, and it's really, really hard."

Poor nurse. She was young and had never had kids. She didn't know what to say. I wasn't excited like most other moms-to-be; I knew what was coming, and I was frightened.

After an awkward moment she rubbed my hands and said, "You can do this. We'll get you through it."

They did.

Norah was perfect and beautiful. I spent a day with her in the hospital, nursing her and feeling motherly. I held her little body and felt God's approval. She came when I was ready, and that was all right. In my mothering weakness, I was given sufficient grace.

As I write now, I'm thirty-six weeks pregnant with my third child. His name is Dale. I was scared to have him, too, until I began to feel his presence on the edges of my spirit. I started to think of him as my athletic, happy son, Dale.

This is not to say I'm completely worry-free about having a baby again. I have forgotten most of the tasks that come with a newborn. I have forgotten how much he's supposed to eat with every feeding, the best way to hold his wobbly head. Used to the heft of my two-year-old, I don't remember newly-born lightness. I can feel him bumping inside me, exploring his narrow world. Other women, when they get to thirty-six weeks, want the baby out. I like him inside, where I can feel him kick without hearing him cry. My body nurtures him automatically. When he emerges in a few days, the nurturing must be deliberate.

But I know I won't be alone. I've felt God's hand guiding me to be the mother, the nurturer, that He called me to be. The care package of mother skills didn't arrive all at once; instead, I'm working with God to unfold those things from within myself.

It helps to stop and look back at how far I've come: I'm not perfect, but I'm better than I was six years ago. And I'm able to better enjoy the blessings of this season of motherhood: the sweet twirling confidence of my little ballerina's dance recital, the delight on my son's face as he figures out how to string one letter's sound onto the next. These are my rewards for the daily diligence motherhood demands. They're not Google-able, but they are real.

I still miss the student side of me; I plan to let her resurface on Google at some point. But nurturing, my primary focus now, does not belong there. Nurturing, I am learning, is inherently private—a gift from God to me, and from me to my children. If my nurturing lost its privacy, it would lose its identity. By embracing the inheritance of Eve's mothering birthright, I received a sacred anonymity: a private, holy grace.

Note

1. Sheri Dew, *Ensign*, Nov. 2001, 96; emphasis in original.

Blood and Milk

Sharlee Mullins Glenn

I dreamed of Oxford . . .

> *(spires, a thousand spires, endless lectures, musty halls*
> *a solitary self in a Bodleian expanse.*
> *A good life, my dear Wormwood. An orderly life.)*

then awakened to laundry
and things to be wiped
(countertops, noses, bottoms)

How did this happen? And when, exactly?

Time flows, it flows, it flows
and there are choices to be made:

left or right?
paper or plastic?

blood or milk?

There's freedom in the bleeding;
bondage in the milk—do not be deceived.

Ah, but it's an empty freedom; a holy bondage—
A sweet and holy bondage.

Five times I chose the chains, those tender chains,
   (though once will bind you just as well!)
and checked the crimson flow.
Suckled while dreaming of Trinity Term
but awakened, always awakened, to the laundry
and to that small and cherished captor at my breast.

Giraffes Kiss

Heather Harris Bergevin

In our house, giraffes kiss. This has been a thought-provoking issue, and not just for my daughter Evva. At twelve months, she began to diligently research animals. First came cats, because of Beo, who has the honor of being her first friend and first word, then Kiki, who was the most amazing animal imaginable. Evva wanted books of cats, pictures of cats, cat toys. Then she met Welkin, and dogs, too, became very fashionable. Suddenly, animal sounds were all the rage. Puppies did not bark at our house, because loud barking was quite startling to our toddler daughter. Instead, they licked and panted happily. Cats said, "Eow." She's very observant— Beo does drop his *m*s.

The toy ark we bought her presents still more challenges. She brings me a sheep; we say, "Baa." She brings me a cow; we say, "Moo." She brings me an elephant, and we trumpet merrily.

Then she brings me a giraffe.

She waits. She brings a sheep and a giraffe together, as if to prompt me. "See," she seems to coax silently. "Sheep says *baa,* giraffe says . . ."

Again she waits patiently, blue eyes confident in my abilities.

I figured becoming a mother would be a pretty intense process. My husband, Noah, and I had already been "trying" for three years, with two miscarriages—and carrying a pregnancy to term was my biggest concern. The chronic illness I'd suffered for years, which limited my energy and mobility, increased my anxiety. And pregnancy itself was daunting enough. During the last trimester with our baby girl, no matter how many books on labor and delivery I read, no matter how many parenting and breastfeeding classes we took, and despite prenatal water aerobics and Lamaze, there was a problem. The gap ratio of necessary-to-acquired knowledge seemed to be spreading daily. How could I get through labor when I couldn't even figure out how to get my shoes tied past my burgeoning belly?

Then the questioning began. "Are you ready?" folks would ask, smirking (the red cloak of the Spanish Inquisition was, I'm sure, only imagined in my late-pregnancy mentality). These were the same folks who, just a few months before—ignorant of my fertility troubles—would comment blissfully, "You guys should have children. You'd be great parents. Don't you *like* children?" Now they snickered menacingly and told birth horror stories while restraining their own preschool-aged terrors.

"Are you ready?" became a clarion call—the bells of family progress ringing in the night. Especially during that 3:00 A.M. potty break with a baby on my bladder.

First came creeping doubts, then growing fears. Could I, as a mother, be enough? Would what I had to give be enough? I was, after all, disabled. None of the parenting books and articles mentioned how to carry a baby when you had to use a cane to walk. I'd read about lots of styles of nurturing, but none explained how to raise a child when you were sometimes home- or even chair-bound.

We were still years away from a useful diagnosis of my illness, but if this route was a struggle for most parents, the learning curve would be even steeper for my husband and me. Being pregnant and disabled was outside the norm. Disabled with a child, or two, or three—well, that seemed like a bit of insanity.

Many women wonder if they can offer their child everything needed. But I already knew I could give much less than they could.

How could my offering suffice?

Were we ready to have a baby? We'd been married for four years. Together, our celestial marriage had weathered three moves (one cross-country), my illness, three years of infertility, two jobs for Noah, buying a home, and many other adventures. We hadn't waited to have children. Now we eagerly anticipated, but also realistically understood the changes about to joyously attack our home. We were as prepared as we could get.

But, ready? Never.

When Evva made her final journey from being an addendum to my body and began fresh as an individual, she was amazing, delightful, beautiful, and more than a little scary. She knew what she needed a lot better than I did. She knew when she was hungry; I had to learn. She knew rather well how to latch on to nurse; I had to learn how to guide her little piranha self. She knew how often she needed to be held (always) and when her best naptimes were (never). She knew what songs she liked on the car radio and which ones made her angry. She knew which glutens made her scream with colic.

Noah and I, on the other hand, knew where to do research, which magazines and books we trusted, which pediatrician was supportive and which one was just not going to work out. We knew which family members to go to for counsel and which were genially insane. We calendared the schedule for her shots and bought a family home evening manual. She, on the other hand, knew that she would feel most safe sleeping not in the other room, but in our bed, curled on Noah's warm chest like a little frog.

We had a lot to learn from each other.

Then her questions started. At first they were easy.

"Dis?" A rabbit.

"Dis?" A ball.

"Dis?" Armed with a pointing finger to roam about her world, and the most important word of all besides *mine,* my little daughter fed the passion for words and trivia she's inherited from her mother. She'd bring me item after item for us to study together—each new flower and toy and book an amazement.

Then came those blasted giraffes. I knew they were only the start.

"This?" War.

"This?" Slavery.

"This?"

As unready as we were to parent one child, the next baby was no less challenging. Of course, we had the gear— thousands of purple and floral blankets, pink eyelet car seats, ladybug decorations, and Disney Princess paraphernalia blooming like sparkling flowers from every corner of the playroom—all the trappings our daughter was rapidly outgrowing. And of course the ultrasound revealed we were having a boy.

As I waded into the water of my second prenatal water-aerobics class, with a small but persistent son clutching my stomach in one hand and bladder in the other, I felt less

ready than ever. Some days Evva sat by the window, begging
me to take her outside. I couldn't until her father got off
work; I wasn't fast enough to catch her little legs in their
eagerness to explore. Her energy and creativity bubbled
around me, while I sat in a recliner, my legs propped.

We watched *Sesame Street* together, took long naps, and
showered. Twice a week in my aerobics class I breathed in
the chlorinated air, stretching my aching legs and back in the
warm water. Together, Noah and Evva went to the park, to
the library, on adventures—all of the things my mother used
to do with me. When she came back I asked if she had fun;
with her face alight with discovered joys she babbled to me
in toddlerese, explaining everything she saw and did.

As this second pregnancy advanced, the questions from
friends began again, with slight variations. "Are you ready for
another child?" they'd say, as if a woman's sixth month of pregnancy is when she begins to think of these matters, not a year
or so before. The switch from one kid to two, they echoed
knowingly—that's the worst one. Are you sure you're ready?

Of course not, we'd whisper in the solace of our own home.
Can you ever be? You can prepare for marriage, but you don't
know what to expect, having never been wed. This is not just
true for us, Noah reminded me; it's true for everybody. Just look
at wedding registries. There'd be fewer table linens and more
cleaning supplies if the bride and groom had any idea what to

really expect. More towels, fewer frilly shower curtains. Not as many party games, and more gift certificates for groceries.

Babies are the same, I figured. Nancy honestly thought she needed the $200 crib set, and then her baby co-slept until she was four, never wetting those Egyptian cotton sheets. Marci really, really wanted all those *Baby Einstein* DVDs, and the little green puppet freaked her little boy so badly he refused to be in the same room.

You can't know until you do it. The trick is realizing that bit. But it would be much worse, I suppose, to truly believe that you're completely ready. The rising panic of realization in those first few hours after the birth of the first—or second, or fourth—would be much worse after thinking in arrogance that you wouldn't have to beg for help regularly from those who did know, at least a bit more, than yourself.

And still, that recurring question crops up in conversation: Are you ready for a second child?

Are you kidding?

I always thought I would be a bubble-blowing, chalk-art drawing, craft-inventing mama. I hadn't envisioned disability, pain, and confusion. Nor had I desired them. My kind husband held me late at night as I lay awake, wanting more for my children than I had energy to give.

But as I worried, Noah reminded me that this, too, was a choice. Not a choice for me to hurt, but a choice to have children despite the pain. Just as important to know in those wee hours of the morning is that each of our children also had a choice—they chose well in their first estate to come to Earth. They might have chosen us as parents, even knowing the trials to come. Surely they knew somewhat of the special difficulties in being a part of our loving home.

There would be no beatings here, but there would be much pain—especially as we discovered more about which illness afflicts me and how it passed through the womb to them. There would not be poverty of things, but poverty of strength. A swingset, but no ability to push them on it; a car, but no ability to drive it to the museum; a stroller, but legs not fast enough to take a whirl around the park; napping, but never enough sleep.

Yet we know they chose to come, and were so eager to do so—and kept trying to come when times were harsh and my womb weak. There can never be any whining that, "Well, I didn't choose to be born."

Yes, you did. You just don't remember.

Someday we'll have a third child, and, I hope, a fourth. With each pregnancy, I gain a little strength, or perhaps more determination to fight this pain, and we definitely gain more knowledge of the illness and more knowledge of ourselves. After the first birth I could walk, tentatively, without a cane. That was a big improvement.

But, ready for more? For any? Can anyone be, ever, in this life?

Once my father tried to explain to me how to be ready. I didn't get all of it, but I remember parts. I was entering my second year of college, still unsure of my focus. We were outside fighting mosquitoes in the Carolina summer as we gently and lovingly stained a sanded dresser in the moonlight.

College, he said, is not to teach you what you need to know for your life. People think they go to college to learn everything they'll need to know, but then they're horribly disappointed later on. They end up working in a job they love, but because it's outside of their major, they feel unqualified. They graduate and have a quarter-life crisis, having spent so much time studying but little learning what they want to do with their lives.

College is *not* for learning all you need, he told me. Rather, it is to teach you how and where to get the information you'll need later, to teach you to keep learning throughout mortality.

Not to learn, but to learn *how* to learn. Especially, for the Saints, to learn the difference between knowledge and Knowledge, to identify the Source of Knowledge. The temple, he explained, is the same—inside we can always gain truth and light, if we know where to look and whom to ask. We learn to be willing to ask, which is perhaps the hardest learning of all.

Whether my little daughter asks her father—or I ask my dad, or my Heavenly Father—the asking opens the door to knowledge. To be willing to learn is, after all, the first step toward learning, as acceptance is the first step toward change. We don't need to know everything in order to be ready to learn anything new.

So, were we ready for our second? Our third? Now? Nope.

We could never be ready.

I, for one, had no idea what sounds giraffes make. (I checked, they're silent. But explain that to a toddler. They also have eighteen-inch purple tongues that are sticky.) Evva finally realized my knowledge of giraffe sounds would forever be lacking. Finding me for the first (but not the last) time insufficient, she chose her own answer.

Giraffes, she decided, would kiss. How this would work as a long-distance call was irrelevant—for now, the giraffes would find one another, be happy in their togetherness, and kiss each other gleefully. As answers go, it's not a bad one.

I still have my own questions about being enough. I'm still disabled. I'm still woefully lacking in housekeeping skills. I'm not very good at crafty things, and I refuse to accumulate the hoard of scrapbooking bits necessary to produce professional results. I can barely knit, and I'm glad there's no dusting-proficiency test.

Mostly, though, I have no idea how to ensure that my children walk in truth, especially in a changeable world with unchangeable Truth. I don't know how to teach them modesty in the midst of nakedness, etiquette within rudeness, to be in the world but not of worldly thoughts and gesticulation. I am daily unsure how to show them a rod that is clearly marked, but sometimes dimly lit or hidden by glaring neon signs pointing toward great and spacious surroundings.

But I do know who holds the answers, and I know how to ask the Teacher my questions, not with a raised hand, but with a bowed head.

How remarkable are the answers that come to mothers for their children—an additional portion of energy to manage vomiting at 2:00 A.M., few hours of sleep yet the ability to function, a little more milk, fewer tears, a great deal more prayer, a little more faith—ounce by ounce, dram by dram, drop by drop. A whisper of comfort in their ear, and even more often, a whisper in my own.

My little ones have more questions. So do I. Together, we search for answers all around us. The mockingbirds nesting outside the window continue to feed their young; bumblebees collect nectar in the spring. The baby giraffe at the zoo, wandering in the streaming sunlight, nuzzles his neck toward his towering mother and—ah! Perhaps they do kiss, after all.

3 A.M.

Heather Harris Bergevin

There are no monsters here, we say,
yet you insist in confidence of five
years' sojourn in mortality—"Dey are."
We soothe, and soon despite my sleepy pat,
and drink of water (twice) and lulling song
you sleep; I lie awake to contemplate
the creaking sounds and shifting of the night.

There are no monsters here, and yet there are
enough to weld the windows, tightly bar
'gainst demons seen or unseen—
for after all,
there is no evil new for worries now,
but that of Incan, Mayan, Holocaust,
Gadianton, and the sins of Cain.
Evil forgot, our doomed past to relive.

Yet Mother's soul will fear no less to fight
dear Wormwood's uncle, half truth, which creates
my enemy of late, insomnia,
or demons worse and difficult to war—
the hotel heiress, idols, stars, who come

to snatch a child away, and notice not,
to walk ever together yet apart
in brilliant circles wander 'til the end.

Hold fast, sweet child in slumber innocent
to tree and rod and fruit that stave away
the sleeplessness of fear
    and I to you
breathe with your breath, and arm about my neck—
Thus peaceful sigh. We sleep on earth as yet,
in desolation sumptuous, and while
there are no monsters here, we plead, but yet
They are.

Grace and Glorie

Lisa Meadows Garfield

I ignored it for years. At first, it was just a nudge, a fleeting thought that would pass through my mind like water through sand. *Adopt.* Then it began to come as a prick to my heart or a flooding warmth in my belly. I knew these signs. I knew they signified some sort of spiritual message, a divine directive. But I wasn't listening and didn't want to. I already had four children by birth, and was happily shifting into the stage of life that isn't dominated by toilet training and naptime.

Finally, the sheer frequency of these promptings compelled me to tell my husband, Stephen, "Honey, I keep having the crazy notion to adopt." I was counting on him to nip this one firmly in the bud.

So I was at once dismayed and excited when he responded, "Oh, no! Me, too!"

We still weren't ready to listen, so we made a list of reasons not to adopt: we were too old, it was too expensive, we had too many kids, it was too much hassle, there'd be too many years devoted to child-rearing. It was an impressive list. We recited it to each other in weak moments.

Life went on, and we tried to pretend we had it all under

control, that we didn't need God's direction quite so directly. Life was good though hectic, and we were stressed, but wasn't that so for all families? I was extremely busy with an intense graduate program, serving as stake Primary president, mourning the sudden loss of three grandparents, and anguishing over our oldest son, who was struggling with drugs and all the concomitant bad behaviors.

But every few months, God would pierce the fog of my frantic mind once more and remind me. *Adopt.*

Stephen and I went over our list again to convince ourselves it was a bad idea.

But when God gets a good idea, He's persistent. And really, we wanted to do the right thing. We had long talks about priorities, about commitment, about how to build a life of value.

We made another list, this one titled, "Why We Should Adopt," to counterbalance the first. But the only thing we could think of to put on our new list was *it feels right.*

In the end, as always, that was enough. The feeling was deep, calm, and touched with grace. We were in accord. We were ready to commit. We researched adoption agencies, chose one, and sent in our application.

We'd come to believe that our family was missing two girls, so we applied to China, since they had lots of baby girls available. As we waited for a referral, I kept seeking divine affirmation of what I already knew was right.

But I felt unsettled; I wanted to *know* my children. Perhaps because they didn't originate with me, grow in me, I needed to know they were mine.

The vision came one summer day while I was visiting my mother-in-law in southern Utah. Sometimes being away from home allows for more quiet time, more intense communication with God, and it was like that on this particular morning, when the kids were playing with cousins and I had some time and space to myself. I moved into a deep, meditative, prayerful state, asking and listening. Suddenly, I saw them both, two little girls with dark hair standing together, as if their life missions could not be fulfilled without each other.

I could feel their spirits. One was gentle and open-hearted, soft and loving. The other was strong-spirited and brave, and her one desire was to give glory to God. Before they were born, before they were mine, I knew them. Grace and Glorie.

Just as our application to adopt was submitted to the agency, China began a massive reform of their adoption policies and procedures. It quickly became apparent that, given our circumstances, it was going to be a long wait, with no guarantees. We were feeling too old to wait.

The agency suggested, "How about Guatemala? We can find you baby girls much quicker there."

We didn't care where they came from. Our only concern was that we find the "right" little girls, the two we felt were destined to be in our family. By this time, we had completely shifted from "control mode" to "faith mode," so we were open to whatever happened.

"Sure," we said. "Let's apply to Guatemala."

It was a Saturday morning in May when we got The Call. I answered the phone to hear Julie, our counselor from the adoption agency, ask, "So, how are you? How's the family?"

It was not unusual for her to check on us periodically as we waited anxiously for our child, so it took me a minute to realize, "Julie, it's Saturday! You never call on Saturday. What's going on?"

"You have a baby daughter," Julie calmly announced. "She's eleven days old. Cute little thing, judging from this picture I have."

I felt myself melting, right there in the kitchen. All the leftover doubt and fear was washed away by a wave of peace so profound that I knew it would sustain me through whatever happened on the rest of this journey. Childbirth is more physically demanding than adopting, and the emotion is all tangled up with the bodily experience. To hear that I was a mother again—to a baby girl three thousand miles away—

excluded me physically, but allowed the emotion of the experience to stand sharply on its own, naked as a newborn babe.

Our daughter's birth mother had named her Julia, then left her in the hospital. Who knows what circumstances prompted such a decision? I credit her for making a plan that ensured her daughter's safety and health. Julia was taken to a foster home run by an expatriate from Ohio, and there she stayed for nine and a half long months.

The wait was agonizing. Every couple of months, we'd get new pictures and post them on the refrigerator. We named our new daughter Julia Grace and included her in all our family plans and prayers. We set up the crib and shopped for baby clothes and bottles. Near Christmas, my sister invited me over one Saturday afternoon with a cryptic message about an "event." I dressed up and drove over, expecting a nice lunch, maybe a movie. But when I opened the door to let myself in, I found my family and friends gathered for a surprise baby shower for Grace. I broke down crying. Later, I sat amongst friends hugging a huge stuffed bunny with a big yellow bow, yearning for my daughter, who remained in Guatemala for her first Christmas.

I tried to be patient, to walk that fine line between being a pest and effectively advocating for my child through the adoption agency. I wasn't very good at it; I just wanted my baby home. Even though I had not yet met my daughter, my heart was drawn to her every single moment. It felt entirely *wrong* to be separated from her. Having birthed children, I knew how it felt to be tightly bonded to a baby. This felt exactly the same.

Finally, all the legal work was complete, and it was time to go pick up our daughter. My husband and I flew to Guatemala City, and there in our hotel room, we met little nine-month-old Grace for the first time. She was old enough to be wary of us and looked alarmed when Helen and Margarita, the only caregivers she'd ever known, left her there with us in the hotel room.

I spread a blanket on the floor and arranged the toys we'd brought all around Grace, who sat still and startled, like an abandoned bird, in the middle of the blanket. She could crawl, but didn't move for a long time. She just sat and watched us watching her, wondering, I'm sure, at this new catastrophe in her young life. Eventually, she got hungry enough to cry, and let us feed her and rock her to sleep. When she woke up, we put her in the bathtub, where she patted the water tentatively, never taking her eyes off of us, the hovering strangers who wouldn't leave.

Within a couple of weeks, Grace must have decided that we were worthy of her trust, because she began to act like she owned us, like any healthy ten-month-old. She slept in a crib in our bedroom so we could respond quickly in the middle of the night to her hunger and fears. I hadn't had a baby to care for in nine years and was delighted to change her diapers, bathe her chubby little body, and dress her up for church. Slowly she began to smile, then laugh, then clap her hands when she saw us. Grace claimed us, called us her own, as we claimed her as our own.

Her older siblings latched onto her immediately. They fought over who got to feed and carry and play with her. The only complaint came the day we lined them all up and explained that because Grace had come home infected with scabies, the entire family had to be treated for it. We handed out bottles of pink lotion and instructed everyone to rub it all over their bodies. We'd repeat this procedure the following week.

My oldest son, Garrett, looked incredulous. "What?" he said. "We have to rub it *everywhere?*" He was nineteen at the time and just making his way back to spiritual health after several years of serious straying.

He responded to Grace with especially deep feeling, as though she were the embodiment of her name. Time and again, I would catch the two of them huddled together in some secret world of their own. Garrett would quietly talk or read to Grace, or the two of them would curl up on the couch, asleep. When we'd go out as a family, Garrett always seemed to have Grace in his arms, while the other kids trotted along beside him, holding her foot. He unabashedly calls her his "favorite." As Garrett worked to turn his life over to the Savior, his little sister served as a representation of the grace he sought.

Near Christmas—one year after the surprise baby shower—Grace was sealed to our family in the Portland Temple. Stephen and I waited with open hearts in the sealing room for our children. When the five of them entered the room, all dressed in white, Garrett carrying Grace and the others holding her feet, I knew that Grace was ours forever.

After Grace, of course, comes Glorie. We had applied for a second adoption as soon as Grace came home, and even before we had all the paperwork in, the agency called with news of our new daughter. Glorie was born as the new millennium rolled around and was referred to our family at the age of five weeks. After we'd received our referral and posted the photo of our beautiful, tiny brown baby on the refrigerator, I settled in for the long, heart-wrenching wait. Things went smoothly this time; we were able to bring Glorie home when she was five months old.

Because I already knew her spirit, I was eager to meet her and get to the business of living for the glory of God. I should have realized that she'd come full of wild energy and unbridled enthusiasm. Though she runs me ragged and stretches my faith in myself, she is pure delight, the personification of

Life. I never fail to see in her a strong, faithful, world-changing woman.

That strong spirit served her well when, at twenty months, she fell and broke her femur. She had to wear a body cast for eight weeks. In the hospital, immobilized in traction, Glorie could hardly stand the aggravation of not being able to move. She pulled her hair out and ripped her face up with her fingernails in frustration. Like a caged bird, she fought to be free. My heart broke for her, and I spent most of two days and nights leaning over her, breathing into her spirit patience and solace. Something happened between us during those two days. A bond of trust formed and solidified into a shimmering, eternal covenant. We belong to each other.

After seven weeks in the body cast, complete with a convenient (though not too sanitary) diapering hole and a crossbar between her plaster-encased legs, Glorie figured out how to walk. The doctors deemed it impossible, though good for her healing leg. At home, we all cheered when she rose and clomped across the living room. Glorie cheers us with her unrelenting determination to live life on her own terms, and I consider it an honor to be her mother.

It has been a sacred privilege to receive the gifts of Grace and Glorie—an ongoing gift, as they infuse our daily life with fun and laughter, with challenge and change. Grace and Glorie have changed the hearts of their older siblings, broadened their love, enlarged their vision of what family means. They've given me and Stephen a fresh look at life and a new opportunity to engage fully in the joy of raising children. I see God's eternal purposes in the faces of Grace and Glorie, and I am unutterably grateful to call them mine.

I have a picture of Glorie's birth mother, Juana. She stands in the lawyer's office by the copy machine, holding her newborn daughter. She looks right at the camera—right at me—though we've never met. Her eyes are full of broken beginnings, but hope and pleading too. I bow my head before my daughter's other mother, acknowledging her loss, accepting her gift.

However our children come to us, even those connected to us by covenant, we cannot claim them as "ours." We are stewards of God's children. We are all, in a sense, adoptive parents, caring for the children of divine parents. To receive with grace the children of Deity, to point them homeward toward glory, is the sacred task of parenthood.

And who can say when it begins? With desire? Conception? Birth? Adoption? Sealing? Each new life, each new relationship is a new beginning.

But the real joy is this: life never ends, love never fails. The journey is eternal.

Indulgence

Heather Herrick

She sleeps on my chest
her breathing steady,
lavender rises and calms my nervousness

For now I can hold her close,
rock her lightly,
keep her safe

It cannot last, will not spoil her . . .

It may spoil me
But I will cherish
her pudgy fingers gently reaching
for a few loose strands of my hair
to soothe herself
to allow sleep to overtake her
as she lies on my chest

I will share my bed with her
While she will allow it

Earthbound

Brittney Poulsen Carman

My daughter has a thing for dirt. As a baby she got into the soil of a mint plant growing in a pot on the living room floor. I took a picture of her dirty face, the muddy smile, and wondered if I should call someone. My mother, our pediatrician, maybe poison control. A nurse friend said not to worry.

"A little dirt never hurt," she said, straight-faced, and, since Stella didn't show any ill effects, I figured I'd take my friend at her word. A sister-in-law confirmed that several of her kids had eaten dirt. Once or twice, she said. It's normal.

Still, in the weeks that followed, a strange ritual ensued. My nine-month-old, in all her crawling, unexceptional coordination, would wrangle the clay pot into a corner behind the sofa and hole up, devouring the black dirt so quickly and covertly that I couldn't stop her. I blamed it on teething and moved the plant. Later, when she lay on her toddler belly near the lemon grass in the garden, shoveling fistfuls of sweet mud into an eager mouth, I realized it was nothing so much as love.

Maybe her taste for earth is an inheritance. As a pregnant woman I craved dirt. I knew it like a need, a fix. My midwife recommended supplements to compensate for the iron leached by the body growing inside of me, but they irritated my stomach, and I didn't like their smell. Once, because they were big and hard to swallow, I let one partially dissolve on my tongue. For two days, my mouth tasted like old tires. I quit taking the pills.

I wanted dirt. During a rainstorm late that summer, I relapsed in a neighbor's flowerbed, falling on a spot of black earth, blooming and blood-red with begonias.

It happened there, I tell myself. Of all the gifts our genes had to offer, hunched and digging, mouth stained dark, that is when I passed this thing on to my child.

My pregnancy was unexpected, which is not to say *unwelcome,* though arguably more startling than something you might plan. Despite being told by our doctor that we might need help trying for a baby, I woke one morning to a queasiness I knew could be only one thing, and sent my husband to the store for a test. I washed my hands before opening it. Nervous, I even wore my yellow rubber gloves, following the directions to the letter. So as not to jinx myself, I closed my eyes while the hormone detection process ran its two-minute course.

The blue line across the indicator read negative. I threw the crummy thing face-up in the trashcan beside the toilet and sulked back into bed. Thirty minutes later, my husband

Andy called me from the bathroom where he'd been shaving. I heard him turn the water off and pull something from the trash. "Honey," he said. "You might wanna come in here. This thing says you're about twenty percent pregnant after all."

Of course a woman doesn't get *twenty percent* pregnant. Still, the pink line bleeding across the indicator was so faint we thought it had to be a trick of light, a pronouncement that the good people at E.P.T. were not entirely willing to make. We called the doctor, who reminded us that the chances were extremely unlikely that I was pregnant, but assured us that we were welcome to come in nonetheless.

His office was unnaturally, arctic cold, and the nurse smelled strongly of flowered lotion. She took the urine sample from me and sent me shivering into the examination room. Andy and I sat holding hands while the doctor explained that I probably had nothing more than a flu virus, my chills were likely from fever, and that it may even be too early for the urine test to tell. He asked how late I was, and I told him that I wasn't. He might have laughed had the nurse not interrupted with this song: "It's positive."

And that was just the beginning of what one might call *the unexpected.* I did not, for example, expect my husband to stand in the doctor's office and cry tears of pure joy. I didn't expect to slump in my seat and mutter a swear word—

though is it really swearing if you can find it in the Bible? I was seasick and blue cold, and I offer myself that excuse.

I did not expect the prayer I whispered, walking through the parking lot, in which I begged God that I would not lose our child. I didn't expect to feel so attached so soon. Nor so emotional. Nor so sick. And certainly, I couldn't expect that shortly after discovering I was pregnant, I would inexplicably, unrelentingly desire dirt.

Some things just can't be explained, but it comforted me to think perhaps my body was simply yearning after some elemental ingredient, something that, really, had been there all along. Fundamentally, aren't we made from the earth? Wasn't it dust the Lord breathed life into and created man? To my unpregnant, sober mind, the logic read a little flawed, but inebriated by the hormones of pregnancy I wondered, who *wouldn't* pilfer the neighbor's flowerbed? Who wouldn't go wanting after soil? Who wouldn't find nourishment among rain-soaked begonias, crinkle-leafed spearmint, sprouting lemongrass and cilantro gone to seed?

Maybe, as my infant turned toddler in the dirt of our garden, the mouthfuls she ate served to connect her to that stuff from which her little body had so recently been created.

Then again, maybe she just liked the taste.

Stella is four now and still taken by dirt. The dirtier the better, though in a pinch she's even eaten sand. Now she eats it less and plays in it more. Add water, and she's made a potion. A little grass, a few pinecones, and she's offering us a stew. Recently, when the *plus* sign on the home pregnancy test announced itself loud and clear, my husband ran from the bathroom to tell Stella. I couldn't make out the entire commotion, but I distinctly heard the ring of her happy cry and Andy saying, "Brother, sister, baby, about the size of a worm."

From there, the two of them sprinted for the garden, where Andy broke dirt with a shovel and Stella pulled skinny, salmon-pink bodies from the soil saying, "This big, Dad? Like this?"

That night, as I stood to lift her from the bathtub, Stella touched my stomach and asked, "Mom, don't you know that worms really do love to eat dirt?"

Tonight it's raining in our small town. It's June, and the air is thick with the smell of soaked pine needles, the rich heft of earth. Holding hands as we walked home from the grocery store today, Stella was content to only stomp in the sidewalk mud puddles. She never bent to slurp from them. She never raised a darkened hand to her mouth. Perhaps she's moving away from that now. Perhaps the dusty point of origin is slipping farther away.

We are spiritual beings, too, after all. But one day, perhaps when she is pregnant with her own child, maybe her desire for dirt will return, surreptitious. I will smile then, and share with her a secret.

She is sleeping. As I write this, the window beside me is open, and I am tempted by the night. The air is cool and rising with the scent of lemon balm, the beguiling, enchanting bouquet of wet dirt.

Perhaps she'll forgive me for sneaking into the darkness a moment without her, for leaving her rowing through her dreams. This need comes unexpected, like the scarlet of a begonia, a thunderstorm in June. If she chances to wake, she would find me feasting in the garden below her window, earthbound, with this speck of something inside me, this fleck of dirt and spirit, becoming heartbeat, and body, and life.

origami birds

Johnna Benson Cornett

birds of intersecting angles,
folded triangles,
suited to the precision of paper and
taking off.

here is the simplest bird
amenable to the smudgy folds of a child.
we mirror make two
as i tell her a story.
we'll put on crayon eyes
completely anthropomorphic.

the only flying is my heart
with a prayer in its beak.

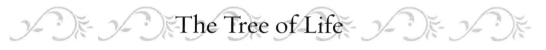

The Tree of Life

Megan Aikele Davies

It was Thursday morning, and I was waiting patiently for my date—my play date. Nathaniel came to play every morning at about nine. We had a wonderful, unique relationship.

I was his mother, and he was my unborn son.

Each morning I arrived at work and ate my breakfast of toast, grapefruit, and hot cocoa. I think Nathaniel loved the hot cocoa as much as I did; he would jump to life soon after breakfast. For several hours he leapt and kicked and swam, and I sat and smiled, taking it all in. I loved these dates, and I couldn't wait for him to come *outside* to play.

That was going to happen really soon, according to the doctor. I had just visited with him the previous afternoon. My due date was just over a week away, and I had dilated to four centimeters. I could go into labor any day. Oh, the joyful anticipation. Only a mother about to deliver knows *that* feeling.

But in the meantime, all my attention was focused on our play dates. Nathaniel was late today, which was unusual—he was generally a punctual little boy. I finished off my breakfast with a Snickers bar, figuring that was enough sugar to make *anyone* come out to play. As the hour wore on and my belly sat motionless, I began to worry a bit. I thought it prudent to pick up my husband and head to the delivery ward of the hospital as soon as I could break away from the morning routine. I was only slightly anxious; sometimes unborn babies like to sleep, and it *was* getting awfully cramped in that little space. I just thought it was better to be safe than sorry.

An hour later, I was in a hospital bed just outside of the nurses' station. A cheerful nurse had checked me in and was routinely setting up the heartbeat monitors on my massive belly. She rearranged the monitors, then rearranged them again, and then again.

She couldn't find a heartbeat.

With a smile on her face, she explained to me that she was new at this, that she was going to send in someone more experienced. Shortly, another nurse came in, equally cheery but more confident in her stride. She, too, struggled to find a heartbeat.

I was just starting to panic when we heard a telltale *thump, thump, thump*—faint, but definitely there. My chest swelled with relief, but it lasted only a moment. The heartbeat, I realized, was my own.

The nurse offered no explanation, but politely excused herself from the room and promised to return promptly. I assumed that my little boy was stressed, and I would certainly be heading to an emergency C-section.

Moments later, a doctor entered the room with an ultrasound machine. As he moved the wand over my belly, I saw the familiar outline of my baby on the fuzzy screen.

Then time froze. I felt as if I had left my body and was watching the scene from another place. There was my husband standing stoically behind me. The nurses had silently flooded into the room, retreating to different corners with expressions of worried anticipation, none daring to get too close. The doctor stared intently at the screen, avoiding my eyes. And I saw myself, young and innocent, waiting to deliver a healthy baby boy.

Then I was jerked back into my skin. I stared at the monitor: there, on the screen, was his little heart, motionless. I watched and waited. Perhaps, I thought, if I looked long enough it would jump back to life.

The doctor gently placed a hand on my leg and said, "I'm sorry. He's gone."

There are moments where you know something very painful is about to happen. A fall from a high place, or a cut from a knife, or a car accident. And there's a timeless space between the moment your brain realizes what is about to happen and the moment you feel it. In that space, you negotiate.

"Perhaps if I brace really hard and spin my head to the left, it won't hurt when that car hits mine."

"Maybe if I hold my finger really tight, I can stop the throbbing that's about to hit."

As I stared at the monitor, I tried desperately to think of a solution. I'd seen situations like this on TV dozens of times: now there would be "Code Red!" shouted over the intercom. More doctors would come. The nurses would rush my bed down the hall to some other place and the magic of modern medicine would happen.

But nobody moved. There was no panicked attempt to resuscitate Nathaniel. He was gone, and for the first time in nine months, I was alone.

For the rest of the world, life returned to business as usual. The nurses all solemnly filed out, heads hung low, to return to their duties. The doctor explained my options. I could deliver Nathaniel then, or I could wait for my body to realize what had happened and begin the labor process on its own. I saw no point in prolonging the inevitable, so I chose to deliver Nathaniel that day. The labor was quick and easy, and Nathaniel was born at 8:00 P.M. on May 20, 2004.

He was beautiful—eight pounds, twenty-two inches long, a mop of dark wavy hair atop his head. He looked just like any other sleeping newborn. But I had the excruciating knowledge that he would never awake, not in this life.

The doctor and nurses were very kind. They treated my little boy as they did any other newborn. The nurses doted over him, tenderly cleaning his little body and dressing him in a tiny white onesie and white booties. They told me how beautiful he was. They showered me with love and with kind words.

I was later told that Nathaniel's death brought a black cloud to the nurses' station that day that didn't leave until I did. Delivery nurses see tragedy of this sort all too often, but for some reason Nathaniel quickly wiggled his way into their hearts just as he had into mine. Perhaps the moment of anticipation they'd all shared with me was enough to make this case more than business as usual. Perhaps they felt a small part of my devastation at the bad news. Perhaps, for just a moment, they had allowed themselves to hope for a miracle along with me, and were also devastated when the answer was no.

* * *

In Dante's *Divine Comedy,* he writes of a place where some souls go after they die. They are not in heaven, and not in Satan's dominion. I think of it as being nowhere.

I spent a week there. It began the morning I left the hospital.

For that week, time stopped for me. I was surrounded by my husband, my parents, my two-year-old daughter, and others who loved me and mourned with me. But I felt separated from them by a giant one-way mirror: I could see them, but I felt they couldn't see me. I felt invisible.

For some reason, staring out the window was comforting. I sat for hours in a rocking chair and watched cars drive by. I couldn't stop. I was never certain if it was day or night, even if I could see sunlight outside. I didn't want to sleep, but eventually I'd collapse in exhaustion. Even then, sleep was fitful. Once, I woke from a nightmare with a panicky feeling that reached all the way to my toes. I sat in bed, trying to sort reality from my dream. But when reality hit me, it was so much worse than the nightmare. I stumbled back to my rocking chair by the window and stared into the darkness.

When a person's brain is severely injured, they go into a coma to allow the brain to heal. Perhaps when we are emotionally injured, it's possible to go into a mental coma. We walk and talk like a normal, functioning human being, but emotionally we're in limbo.

Questions plagued me, tormenting my rational mind. Where did Nathaniel go? "A better place"? What does that mean? What is he doing there? Is he sad he had to go? Will I see him again? When? What if I forget how to love him before then? What if he doesn't love me when I get there? Does he know he's a part of our family?

My thoughts were stuck in a continuous figure-eight. I'd think through each question, and once I had pondered them all, they would start again at the beginning.

I'd always been a deeply religious person. But it's one

thing to believe in the theory of heaven and hell, in salvation and eternal families, and another thing to trust that the spirit of your child is alive and safe, that you will absolutely see them again. My week in emotional limbo was a crucible of faith. I needed time to think through what I had always been taught and what I really believed.

Despite my mental state, there was work to be done. I was still Nathaniel's mother, and for the next week I had duties to perform. Laying Nathaniel to rest was the only service I would provide for him in this lifetime, and I put what little energy I had into planning his funeral. I carefully picked out a beautiful, white crocheted sleeper for him to be buried in. We purchased a small, wooden casket—smaller than my daughter's baby doll bed. I pored over the Primary *Children's Songbook* to find songs for his graveside service.

I was propelled by the thought that I'd still get to see him several times. I waited for these moments with all the anticipation that a child saves for Christmas morning. My husband and I went to the funeral home to go over funeral options, and they graciously brought us our little boy and allowed us to be alone with him for about ten minutes. A few days later, we dressed him for burial.

Every time I was allowed to see his body, I had to suppress a strong urge to grab him and run. From the moment he was born, people kept taking my son from me—the nurses, the mortician, and now the funeral-home employees. I couldn't help but feel that if I could get him away from all of them, I'd finally get to keep him. But rational thinking always returned, and I realized that *death* had taken him away. Everyone else was just doing his or her job.

Of all the terrible moments that week, closing the casket right before we buried him was the worst of all. I knew for certain then that I'd never see him again in this lifetime. There was nothing more to look forward to. There was no more hope.

*   *   *

We buried Nathaniel on a Friday morning in the pouring spring rain. My husband carried Nathaniel's small casket from the limousine to his final resting place. Our young daughter frolicked in the rain while the rest of us sat somberly under a small canopy. My husband and I both spoke briefly and we sang some children's songs. I lingered anxiously after the dedication of the grave until the chill of the rain reminded me to leave.

The next day, the sun came up, and my life continued, but I wasn't a willing participant. My emotional pain was intense. The monotonous tasks of life seemed meaningless. I struggled to reach out to my daughter and my husband. I spent many hours on my knees begging God to shore up my broken heart—I felt like my heart had an actual tear in it, gaping and sagging.

As the days and weeks wore on, I grew stronger and stronger, as if somebody had built clumsy scaffolding underneath my heart and it was slowly, but surely, being lifted back into place.

I knew this healing was not a result of my own will. As I pondered how it was possible, the Spirit taught me that I was being literally lifted by the prayers of others—many others. I could almost hear their voices. Every time the grief of my loss would wash over me, I would soon feel the collective spirit of others carrying me above it and moving me forward.

The pain didn't go away, but I was able to endure it.

In the months that followed, I was continually blessed by the Spirit, even as I grieved. I learned more about life and God and our purpose here than I had in my previous twenty-seven years. Through hours of pondering, I realized that pregnancy and delivery can teach us a great deal about Christ's love for us. When we conceive life, we sacrifice all we have to another being—our oxygen, our nutrients, our health, our energy. When we deliver a child, we spill our own blood that another may have life.

As I looked back on my pregnancy with Nathaniel, I saw every ache, every pain, and every sickness of those nine months as a part of the miracle. More than ever before, I understood why mothers gladly do it over and over again. And I resolved that I would do everything I could to have more children, despite the risks that I now knew on such a personal level.

*   *   *

It has now been several years since Nathaniel so quickly returned home. Time has brought perspective and lasting peace. I know now that his death was not a tragedy; rather, it was simply a part of the eternal relationship we enjoy as mother and son. My grief is part of my love for him, and this is how it should be.

The love we hold for our children is not meant to die when they do. It is an *eternal* love. It connects us here on Earth, and it also connects us across the veil of death. The sealing power of the priesthood officially binds us together forever, but it is the love we have in our hearts that binds us together in spirit and brings us joy in eternal life.

On Nathaniel's headstone is an illustration of the tree of life. The symbol helps me understand every aspect of Nathaniel's birth and death. I chose it partly because I wanted to somehow capture my feelings that Nathaniel is still a part of us. He has the same roots as my other children, and he will always be a part of our family tree.

Apart from the obvious symbolism of a tree, I love the

spiritual meaning behind the tree of life. It is a symbol of the love of God. As I grieved, it was the love of God that helped me endure those endless moments. As I healed, it was the love of God that pieced me back together and made me whole again. Now, it is the love of God I feel in my heart every day that brings me lasting peace and joy in spite of the tragedy I have experienced in the past. And, perhaps most importantly, it is because of the love of God that Nathaniel is an immortal being and that we can someday enjoy eternal life as a family.

In Lehi's vision, he reaches the tree and longs almost immediately for his family to join him. He wants them to find the joy he has found in partaking of the fruit. Without them, his joy cannot be full.

I know a little of how he must have felt. My greatest goal is to live this life worthily so that I might also, in death, reach the tree of life. It wouldn't be complete without every member of my family joining me there. I picture Nathaniel already waiting under its shade, beckoning to our family to join him.

Perhaps part of the miracle of his birth and death is the motivation he provides me and my family to be worthy of rejoining him. In the meantime, I'm still happily waiting for our play date that will last forever.

Intent to Do Good

Ailene Long

And after ye have obtained a hope in Christ ye shall obtain . . .
the intent to do good—to clothe the naked, and to feed the hungry, and to
liberate the captive, and administer relief to the sick and the afflicted.
—Jacob 2:19

It's 7:15 Monday morning. I'm on my knees on the hard-wood floor, searching for Preschooler's socks under my bed, where my dear husband kicked the clean laundry. The uncomfortable maneuver is made more difficult by Second Grader hanging on my shirt chanting, "I need food, I need food," echoed by the hungry cries of Infant in my arms. Fourth Grader unloads a barrage of faulty logic at me, trying to convince me that she should stay home from school even though she has no symptoms of illness.

I try to tune them all out but still hear the questions and complaints racing through my mind—*Why am I doing this? I hate it!* I want to spend my life doing something that really helps people, something meaningful, like Gandhi, Mother Teresa, or Martin Luther King Jr. did. I can't believe my best intellect and creativity are needed to find socks.

And then I remember . . .

Over-bright Wyoming sun bears down on my shoulders, rays so hot they feel heavy, weighing me down. So bright, I squint at my bleached-out surroundings—the dried-up lawn in the teeny yard of our decrepit rental home, the neighbors' worn houses. How did a girl like me end up in a place like this? A few months earlier my husband and I were both full-time students. Finishing my degree had been important to both of us, so we shared housekeeping and child-care responsibilities equally. Our toddler had perched on Shane's hip as he taught undergrad geology courses, and had frolicked on a blanket in the middle of my medieval Spanish literature study group. It worked.

I graduated, and Shane accepted a summer internship with a "real" oil company in this place. I gladly followed with our two-year-old child and my seven-month-pregnant self. We drove off on a sunny day, leaving behind our equal-student personae as we entered this small town in our new roles as a nine-to-five breadwinning man and his seven-months-pregnant, stay-at-home wife. I hadn't thought any of this through—I didn't realize we were *both* interns for the summer, trying out our future careers.

One day, the mosquitoes feasted on my shins, bringing me back to the task at hand—standing in the teeny yard, trying to hang out to dry the mountain of wet laundry that balanced on my shoulder. The mosquitoes were murder, but swatting them was impossible. The Largest Pregnant Belly the World

Has Ever Seen and the shooting sciatic pain it caused made bending over nearly impossible. It was the middle of July, the hottest week of the year, and I'd already passed a miserable half hour in the antique house with no air conditioning, washing dishes by hand in hot, soapy water, wondering if the trickle tickling the side of my neck was sweat, condensation of the steam coming off my hands, or tears of frustration.

I finally got the two-year-old asleep for a nap, and somehow dragged the million-pound hamper of wet clothes out of the car and into the yard without going into labor. By that time, I was almost in tears again. This was my job; I wanted so badly to do it, to feel capable, but I had no idea it would be so hard. I had no idea it would hurt so much.

I got a few items on the line and took a minute to balance on one foot (like *The Karate Kid,* or a very large flamingo) to scratch the shin of one leg with the heel of the other. I moved slowly, trying not to drop the clothes, trying not to drop the clothespins, trying not to spark the sciatica. Success! Both feet back on the ground, I moved to hang the next item. Crisis! In slowest motion my foot came down wrong on the uneven turf, and turned under. I shifted my weight to avoid a sprained ankle, and the clothespins flew out of my hands. I grabbed at them, knowing I wouldn't be able to pick them up if they fell.

The sudden shift was in the wrong direction, and sciatica

pains shot down my leg like an electric shock. The clean, wet clothes flew off my shoulder into the dust. Seriously afraid of falling now, I grabbed the clothesline and managed to right myself, but at the cost of the clothes already hung. My grab bounced them off, and they landed in the dust with the rest. I was upright and whole, but the clothespins and laundry were all over the place, the yard littered with debris from the Battle of the Laundry. Which I had lost.

I retreated into the shade of the house and found myself on my knees, in tears. The crying wasn't the polite upset of a pregnant woman, but the deep wracking sobs of a soul wrestling with the purpose of life.

It was so hard—the all-encompassing, overwhelming business of being pregnant, taking care of the home, the children, the family. It was impossible! No one could do it all. And how could there be time for anything else? How would I ever make a contribution to society? How would I ever live the gospel? I wanted to "feed the hungry, clothe the naked, visit the sick and administer to their relief" like Mother Teresa and my other heroes. But how could I ever do all that if I couldn't even get the family's underwear clean?

I asked my burning questions but didn't expect a reply. One came anyway. In my mind I heard a voice repeating that same scripture, Jacob 2:19, but this time it was accompanied by memories of what I'd done that day. I saw myself again struggling to clean the dishes in the stifling kitchen and understood that to be a part of "feeding the hungry." My entire struggle with the laundry was part of "clothing the naked." Kissing my two-year-old's hurts was definitely "administering to [her] relief." And then I thought of the baby I would soon give birth to, and really considered how naked, hungry, and helpless he would be. Without feeding, clothing and care, he wouldn't make it.

I felt assured that while the world surely benefited from the work of Mother Teresa, my mothering contributed too. I was astounded as the mental light went on. Service was not something to get to when my work was done; my work was a way to serve.

It's 7:18, the same Monday morning; everyone is still loudly voicing their needs, and I don't have time to reminisce any longer. But those few moments will do to remind me of the clarity of purpose I felt on a hot Wyoming July afternoon, when I gratefully re-committed to being a mom. With a slightly improved attitude, I forge on to find the socks, make breakfast, check a temperature, and do all that a mother does.

"The most important of the Lord's work you and I will ever do will be within the walls of our own homes."[1]

NOTE

1. Harold B. Lee, *Stand Ye in Holy Places* (Salt Lake City: Deseret Book, 1974), 255; emphasis added.

Ice and Fire

Melissa Young

Ice
A frozen landscape—
Unbending, mundane—
the sparkling, brittle surface
of my life.

I swirl beneath the rigid ice,
Soul-burning with ambition,
Breathing dreams that bubble
    forth
At the edges of the day.

Yet I fear the distracting cracks
And quickly snuff the flame.

The ice, you see, must safely
    bear the weight
Of children's souls.

They move freely above
—laugh, slide, dig, scrape—
secure in the frosty sameness.

I churn silently beneath;
waiting for the spring of
    agedness,
the heat of long experience,
to melt the elements of reality
into one fluid body.

Fire
Softly I blow
on the embers of self
beneath the ash
of crumbled skill,
coaxing warmth to ward
the chill of emptiness.

My children gather around,
curious to see the flame.

Tiny hands reach
toward the heat.
Tinder hearts kindle
with sparks of passion and joy.

They crackle, dance.

While I,
singed by the blaze of possibility,
step back
to watch them
glow.

Creation out of Chaos

Heather Herrick

It's 9:30 on a Monday morning. I look around to consider everything I need to do in the next fifteen minutes before we have to be out the door to take Margaret, my four-year-old, to preschool. She and Cole, her eighteen-month-old brother, sit at the small table in the corner of our living room, which doubles as the dining room, triples as the play room, quadruples as the family room, and quintuples as a guest bedroom for visitors (here in our 500-square-foot New York City apartment, everything is multipurpose).

As they eat their breakfast, I step over a pile of Tupperware from Cole's latest cupboard-emptying project and decide that putting these away is not one of the things that *needs* to be done before we leave. Passing the mirror, I add brushing my hair to the list of non-needs, pull the tangled mess back into a ponytail, and rush to find baby wipes, sippy cups, umbrellas (in case the weather forecast holds true), Margaret's shoes, the lesson plan I'm teaching, house keys, subway card, and cell phone.

I pause for a moment at the computer desk, where my phone is charging, and consider tucking my writing notebook and pen under my arm. The notebook is right where I left it last night, with only a few brief ideas for an essay scratched onto one of the pages. For months now I've been intending to write about this season in my life, to capture the flavor and cadence of my days. I bought myself this notebook and declared it to be strictly for *my writing*. The prospect of using my time and energy to do something that wouldn't get undone fifteen minutes later enticed me.

Yet despite my desire to write, my notebook is all but empty. I figure I won't be able to remedy that while teaching preschool, so I leave the notebook on the computer desk, hoping naptime will afford me the couple of hours I need to really get started. Feeling a bit discouraged, I remind myself that I can make this happen. I can do more than restack the Tupperware: I am an intelligent, insightful, creative person.

However, the clock that lights up on my phone as I pull it from the charger reminds me I need to hustle if we're ever going to make it to preschool on time. And as usual, today's "must-do" tasks muscle their way into my mental schedule and obliterate any writing time I try to set aside. Refocused on getting out the door, I grab the stroller from the other corner of the living/dining/play/family/guest room, unfold it, and begin loading everything I've just gathered into the basket underneath and the pockets on back.

Stroller's original purpose: push child from point A to point B. Stroller's New York purpose: push child, books, jackets, umbrellas, toys, snacks, rocks, twigs, flowers and leaves your daughter decides are treasures, from point A to point B.

Suddenly Margaret screams, "Cole got my princess!"

Cole calls, "Down, down, down." I look up just as he chucks the last of his uneaten cereal from the bowl and holds up a plastic princess figurine in his other sticky hand. Determined to be on time, I take a deep breath, use a paper towel as a washcloth for Cole's hands and face, then as a mop for the cereal. I move him from the highchair to the stroller and toss Margaret's shoes to her. After Cole is strapped in, I promise Margaret she'll get the princess back as soon as she has shoes on her feet. Sniffling, she complies, and Princess Aurora makes it safely back into her hands.

On our way out we pass my unmade bed in the room that doubles as a gym and triples as a home office. I shrug and mentally add "make bed" to the list of things that don't *need* to be done this morning.

It's now 9:45 A.M. and we'll probably make it to preschool on time, if the subway train comes soon. One day we waited, with hundreds of agitated, hot, and angry riders for forty minutes, even though the schedule says a train will come every ten. Unreliable time schedules aside, there are many things I love about the NYC subway system. For one, I do not have to park, change oil, put gas into, or pay for a car.

Plus, it's affordable and extensive. Sure, it could use more ramps and elevators for mothers like me who carry a fifteen-pound stroller loaded with a thirty-pound toddler down the stairs to the train platform and back up to the street again, but it gets us where we need to go and even provides a means of education and entertainment.

I admit the education sometimes comes in unusual ways. This morning, Margaret wants to know why that man next to her has a cartoon character holding a gun tattooed on his forearm, and how I know the person across the train is a girl and not a boy. As I struggle to come up with tactful answers, some hip-hop boys enter the train. I breathe a sigh of relief at this welcome distraction and whisper, "Let's watch these boys dance." One of them cranks up his portable stereo; two others begin to dance. Wearing T-shirts that hang down past the knees of their baggy sweats, hair pulled back by black doo-rags, they perform an intricate hip-hop routine with incredible energy. They make impossible back flips, just missing the tightly bundled woman standing close to the door. They take tight spins in the two square feet of empty space between passengers.

When the music ends, we all clap, and the dancers pass through the train with their oversized shirts stretched out for donations. Margaret insists we give them some money, and Cole claps along with everyone else. I willingly dig for some quarters in my purse, impressed by the dancers' ability to create something within the chaos of this moving, crowded train.

We arrive at preschool right on time. It's a co-op school formed by moms in my neighborhood; the seven of us rotate responsibility for teaching, assisting, and babysitting. It's fun and free (if you don't adhere to the "time is money" adage). The four boys and three girls in our class have really put me to the test. When it's my turn to teach, I've learned to prepare short lessons and activities to avert the spontaneous running, screaming, and chasing games that easily erupt. Together we sing, run, read, jump, match, run, dance, and then sing again. I feel a few moments of relief mingled with success.

After preschool I choose our other common form of transportation to get home. It is not a minivan with car seats, a radio, and heater/air conditioning. Nope, we walk on the legs and feet God gave us. On the way home the stroller fulfills another of its New York duties: grocery cart. I stop by the corner store and pick up bananas, bread, and two gallons of milk. When I said I love transportation in New York because I don't have a car to worry about, I wasn't thinking about times like these, when the load of groceries hanging off the back of the stroller adds another twenty pounds of weight. The experts say I should have more energy and a longer life due to these treks, but in the moment I don't exactly feel grateful.

Cole gets the lucky ride in the stroller, but Margaret walks alongside me. She likes to look around, sing, explore. However, today I am trying to speed up the process of getting home. After a morning full of domestic engineering, I am eager to start writing my essay. I encourage Margaret with reminders of how strong and healthy she is. This works for a few minutes, but things get more desperate as every few steps Margaret starts again with, "I'm tired of walking."

"Let's pretend we're riding our ponies," I say. We've ridden them many times before. Hers is named Rainbow Dash (a name she came up with herself, which is fitting for a pony that has rainbow-striped hair) and mine is named Chocolate (Choco for short, and by this point I could really use some). Even the riding of such fine ponies hasn't taken the whine out of walking today, so I resort to bribery. "Stop whining and you can have a lollipop when we get home." When this tactic fails, I switch to a threat: "Stop whining or you can't watch *Dora* in the morning."

I'm not proud of these tactics, but it's much more difficult to be creatively patient and encouraging when my heart rate is reaching 180 on the final stretch of hill up to our apartment. *Remember how strong and healthy you are!* I think to myself. *Giddyup, Choco, let's make it a run and not a saunter or no pony snacks! We want to get there today and not next week!* Threatening a pretend pony has got to be healthier than threatening a three-year-old.

To Margaret's delight, I drop her and her pony off at a friend's apartment for a play date. Cole, who has fallen asleep in the stroller/grocery cart, gets carried up the stairs along with the milk. I move him to his bed for an afternoon nap. It's now 1:30 P.M. I look around at all the things that didn't need to be done this morning and consider everything that I should do before Cole wakes up in a couple of hours. My unmade bed calls to me from the bedroom/gym/home office, beckoning me to take a nap. Determined to create something permanent, I ignore the books that have been pulled off the shelf and the sticky cereal residue on the floor. I wade through the Tupperware and toys, past my bed, and sit down at the computer. Finally! My moment for creativity has come.

But now that my moment is here, I don't know what to write.

I glance over the list of ideas in my writing notebook and stare at the blank white screen with the cursor blinking, waiting. Uninspired, I think about the boys dancing on the train, hoping to channel some of their creative talent. Surely I can work them into this essay somehow. I begin to describe their dance, their wardrobe. Other images from this muddled morning of mothering begin to come: multi-purpose apartment living, paper-towel mops, clever tactics to curious questions, stroller grocery carts, colorful and not-so-colorful ponies.

As I type I realize my creativity hasn't been used up by the must-do tasks of my daily life. On the contrary, the colors, limits, vibrancy, and rhythm of this city life as a mother have given me the raw materials to practice the process of creation over and over again.

And right now I'm taking the opportunity to use the chaos as a tool instead of an excuse. I record some of what I've created today: a clean floor, a preschool experience, a happy memory with my daughter, a stocked refrigerator, a convenient place for my son to nap. In the final minutes before Cole wakes up and Margaret's play date is over, I finally complete the essay I've wanted to write for months: a record that will endure, even after the books get pulled off the shelf again, the groceries get eaten, and hip-hop boys exit the sliding doors of a crowded subway train.

no time

Johnna Benson Cornett

pressed
for the sleeping and eating,
care of the young and
the sleeping and eating,
duties of shelter,
to keep it clean and warm
and lit and locked and live,
and all the wordless aspects
of errands and urgencies,
without details, lacking words,
and the sleeping and eating
and

no time.
no time to hold it all
in a net spun of my breath,
greater than my arms.
no time
for structure of words
pronunciation of dream
a home for the future
like an egg from my mouth,
an incomplete magic.
no time for the keening of my
    heart,
my wistful whispers, my love,
my hoped-for ghost
reach beyond reaching
no time.

no time
for the first gift

upon Adam and Eve,
speaking, even in paradise,
to each other and god.
what comfort then,
even before suffering.

the gift not given
to dumb beasts
pressed in their
eating and sleeping,
care of the young,
and muted thoughts.

no time for
the trailing touch of love,
and talk, like castles and ships
made of smoke
that rises together.
where is my home?
where is my resting hope place?
no time.
no time.

Make me some time.
knit it of yarn.
spin it of lint
collected from corners.
woolgather,
gather me.
knit me a covering—
shirt sweater shawl.
wrap me in your time.
wrap me in time.

Natural-Born Mother

Maralise Petersen

When I welcomed my first baby home, he suckled my untapped breast, cradling his arm around my soft back and opening his mouth as if gulping sunshine. The hand-me-down couch where we cuddled was soft and warm, the December chill kept safely outside by the thick insulation of our 1920s bungalow and a thermostat turned high enough to make the devil sweat. Meals and gifts came in; soiled diapers and wrapping paper went out. I nursed by the light of our Christmas tree, where five-pointed stars illuminated the exhaustion and the miracle of mothering an infant.

I loved my son's gorgeous nursery, his little outfits. He had matching hats for each ensemble. Heck, he had matching hats for each set of pajamas. I felt confident in my ability to change his diapers, clean up his spit, read to him at night, teach him to eat and sleep. My transition to motherhood felt natural; I met his needs, and that service met mine. One night as I cuddled my baby in the rocking chair, my husband looked down at us and casually asked, "How many children do you want?"

I looked at my tiny baby's longer-than-life eyelashes, his

ideal face, his beautifully formed body and softly said, "Many. So many."

My son and I spent two joyful and insulated winters together before I learned about the upcoming arrival of a second son, a surprise this time. I wasn't ready. My husband was excited, assured of our ability to handle another child. But my thoughts were less confident, more burdened by our recent cross-country move, our financial dependence on savings and student loans, and the distance from any kind of family support.

In tandem with my fears for this new baby, my older son's daily activities lost their magnificence. Instead of feeling awestruck, I felt tired—tired of his constant needs, of the daily routine, overwhelmed by new behavioral problems and the sometimes rocky transition to toddlerhood.

And then I started to have contractions. With the beginnings of labor—many weeks too soon—I sensed a change in myself and my son and my life.

"He doesn't suck very well," I told my husband shortly after getting home from the hospital with our small-but-healthy baby boy.

He dismissed it. And so did I. We assumed it was just another indication of the differences in our sons. My older son was dark-haired, amazingly resilient, and strong. My new baby was blond and felt fragile, sensitive. I continued to nurse my youngest and gradually adjusted to his "style" of nursing.

But at six months old, he lost his tenuous position on the growth charts, and we found blood in his stool. The emergency room doctor advised us to visit a gastroenterologist. The pediatrician ran blood tests. Everything came back normal.

"If he doesn't start to gain weight," he told us, "I'll have to diagnose him with 'failure to thrive.'"

Three months later, the doctor did.

That's when we began seeing specialists. I found myself dragging two "babies" to doctors that took months to get into and hours to travel to and from. My older son didn't hold up well under the strain. His behavior at home was difficult, but in public, it was almost unbearable. He threw fits on the trip, in the waiting room, and while I was talking to the doctor. We ate in cars and slept in waiting rooms. We moved. Again.

The fatigue I'd experienced during pregnancy felt like a long-lost vacation.

"Don't step on your brother's head. *Ever. Again!*" I heard the words being screamed out of my mouth but wasn't fully aware of what I said. I sobbed and rocked my baby, hoping there was no brain damage. My two-year-old couldn't have known that jumping on his brother might hurt him permanently. Or that his constant temper tantrums were more than my insufficient patience could take. He didn't understand that his little brother was sick, that his mom was becoming sick with fear and worry—worry for her own emotional health, for the well-being of her older "difficult" child, for the continued growth of her younger "fragile" child.

In that first (and unfortunately not the last) time I lost control with him, I realized I *wasn't* a natural mother. I was an inadequate mother. I was a desperate mother. As my son's behavioral issues escalated, so did my desperation. Motherhood had seemed so easy once, when I knew what he needed and how to give it to him.

Now I was in the dark, not knowing how to feed one child and how to love the other.

As the months passed, my despair deepened. My younger son was still not gaining weight; he had no curve on the growth charts. Yet we could find no reason. The results from our visits with the neurologist, the cardiologist and the first gastroenterologist were inconclusive. Each doctor "cleared" him and said to feed him more—as if I hadn't tried that already.

The pulmonary specialist was the next on the list. We saw her before our appointments with the second gastroenterologist, the endocrinologist, and the geneticist. It was there in the pulmonary specialist's office that the tide began to turn. It was there that this doctor shared a non-clinical, non-medical secret with me.

She shared it before doing a cystic fibrosis test, before the geneticist recommended a test for Williams Syndrome and a skeletal study, before the second gastroenterologist ordered an emptying study, a barium swallow, an upper GI, an endoscopy, countless blood tests, and before the allergist wanted a fifty-prick allergy test.

This wise and caring doctor said that if I really felt that something was wrong with my son, despite the lack of clinical evidence so far, then there *was* something wrong. It was just a matter of finding out what.

She was right, and so was I.

Her advice made me realize that I was gifted. Not with the miraculous knowledge of my son's needs, not with more ability than his medical caretakers, but with a God-given sense that if anyone was going to help my son, it had to start with me.

My confidence and persistence paid off when, two years after beginning our search, we received the first of three diagnoses. My son was diagnosed with reflux; then eosinophillic esophagitis, a rare allergic disorder; and then celiac disease.

I wish I could say we found the cause and solution for the problems with my older son. He is now five and still throws fits in doctor's offices, grocery stores, and even more at home. My patience often grows dim before the sun is fully awake. And with all of the worries that surround my younger son, my deepest fears are for the older "healthy" one.

I've learned that instead of sending him to time out for melting down on the ball field, what he really needs is something no behavioral book has recommended, no other parent has suggested.

He really needs me to love him anyway—love him so much that his outbursts are only a small part of the beautiful and gifted person he is. He needs me to see him as more than the sum of his bad behaviors. Sometimes it seems he needs more love than I have to give. But I also feel my capacity expanding. And that gives me hope for my son—and for myself.

I hope that if I won't give up on him, he won't give up on me.

And so we move forward in the only way we know how. In the mornings, the roar of the blender wakes the kids up as I puree my younger son's calorie-boosted breakfast. The night-time Pediasure bottle sits on the counter, and for a moment I feel guilty that my three-year-old "baby" still drinks from it. But then I remember that it took me a year to get him to ingest those vitamin-fortified 8 ounces, and I need to be grateful for every drop he takes.

After the blender finishes its job, the toaster pops up with my older son's frozen waffles. We all march into the living room where the TV is already on. We do mouth-training exercises with my younger son to strengthen his eating muscles, set a timer, then force him to eat, encouraging every small step and ignoring every loud protest. We turn the TV off and on to encourage his bites. Sometimes he eats, sometimes he throws up, sometimes we give up and instead laugh at the TV. His older brother alternates between "helping" (which usually means forcing his dictatorial desires on all) and ignoring us, only to throw a fit when the TV flicks off.

This is not the way a "natural" mother would feed her kids. Maybe a better term would be a hard-working mom, a perseverant mom, or more accurately, an imperfect mom raising imperfect kids.

A very average mother growing stalks of wheat out of the broken ground of her greatest fears.

Sometimes I feel guilty that motherhood hasn't come more naturally to me, that my kids aren't more "normal." Sometimes I want to go back in time to those peaceful days when my first son was an infant, when everything seemed ideal.

But other times I realize how unrelenting and how unkind "ideal" can be, and how joyful my less-than-ideal children are. Without one son's behavior problems, I wouldn't have learned that empathy and kindness are sometimes the only discipline strategies that work. Without my other son's health concerns, I wouldn't have learned how kind his big brother can be to a sibling in need. I wouldn't know how beautiful it is to see an empty bowl or how inspiring it is to hear a small mouth say, "I did it!"

I can't say that I'm a natural mother. That would be a lie. But in being a not-so-natural mother, I've learned that "natural" is not what my kids need. They need more than that, more than easy, more than routine.

They need me, and the person they are helping me to become.

we all hate to be alone

Johnna Benson Cornett

we all hate to be alone, oh my child.
i feel your heart knock against my hand,
your shrieks to my shushes; i am here,
yours, so sleep in your little bed.
you may let go of the world; it is here,
it is yours, still, sleep awhile.

we all hate to be alone, we should be trees,
our branches espaliered, in a grid,
and small birds rocking on our hands,
birds shaped by the patting of palms.
we should be twined together, earth and sky.
i am yours, connected; sleep awhile.

we all hate to be alone; so do i,
the bowl of your toothless mouth
opens in its red-pink cry:
this is how we shut one another out,
lost in a maelstrom of dissatisfaction.
i am here, outside; sleep awhile.

we all hate to be alone, and for that
you are always found on my fingers,
your pale hair, the clench of your hand,
the pleasant folds of your limbs,
the dance of caress, all day long.
i am here, let go; sleep awhile.

Will It Ever Be Enough?

Felicia Hanosek

"Will it ever be enough?" I complained under my breath. "The Sabbath is *not* a day of rest." My head pounded. My arm, holding the baby, was about to fall off. My ears—and heart—burned with the "constructive criticism" offered by the well-meaning previous Primary president.

The music leader was a no-show, and the bishopric counselor—who never seemed to get around to calling Primary workers—cheerfully informed me that the eleven-year-old Scout leader was being taken for another position. My sluggish brain, a consequence of a late-nighter working on handouts, refused to supply the requisite "Sunday smile."

I looked for my husband and found him up the hallway conversing amiably. Our two-and-a-half-year-old was noticeably absent from his arms. Though I never expressly asked, I'd expected him to pick her up from nursery—he hadn't, again. AARGGGGGH! I stomped to the nursery room, grumbling to myself. It was the same old story.

When would I get a rest?

Juggling family needs, housework, service, and personal fulfillment always left something undone. It was even harder to feel at peace with what I *was* able to do. Sundays were regularly the biggest challenge. Often, after putting on a great show at church (the never-ending smile, keeping children reverent during sacrament meeting, signing every sign-up sheet, displaying attractive laminated visuals, and putting out all organizational fires) I found my talents and energies spent. I had nothing but a grumpy wife and mom left for the family. The car ride home often set the unhappy tone: tired kids whining or crying, Mom snapping, and everyone wondering what—or if—we would eat once we got home.

I knew this was not what the Lord wanted for me or for my family, but no matter how hard I worked, there was always more to do. I wondered, "How will I ever know if I am doing enough?"

Being a list-oriented person, I decided I needed a better list. If I could figure out what mattered most and concentrate my efforts there, I reasoned, I might feel more settled inside. To find my priorities—my balance—I spent several months pondering and praying, reading the counsel of prophets and apostles, and fasting.

The collection of teachings and inspirations reached critical mass: I knew what my priorities should be. They were based on my talents, my responsibilities, and my earthly mission. The priorities commanding my greatest attention were my relationships with God, spouse, and children. Homemaking, Church callings, and relationships with extended family and friends came next. Continuing education,and hobbies such as piano, gardening, and reading rounded out my grand list.

But knowing my priorities was just the beginning. I still couldn't accomplish everything. The perfectionist in me required nothing less than 100 percent. However, if I gave 100 percent to everything on the list, I would implode. And if I didn't give 100 percent, I would have to endure harsh self-judgment and, perhaps, the equally harsh judgment of others.

For example, homemaking was number four on my priority list. Thus, if someone dropped by unannounced they would observe that I suffered from CHAOS (Can't Have Anyone Over Syndrome).[1] I didn't want to be judged to be a lazy slob. Likewise, my Church calling was number five on the grand list. Church service, like housework, was never done; there were always people to visit, casseroles to make, and lessons and visuals to construct. If I gave 100 percent to Church service, higher priorities such as relationships with God and family would suffer. Yet if I didn't give 100 percent, someone might criticize my lack of talent or work ethic.

I wanted the accolades and recognition of my outward "perfectness" (from ward members, neighbors, and even from the Lord), but inside, I knew I couldn't do it all. And I didn't know any other way to find peace and self-worth.

I finally began to understand, paradoxically, as I became even busier as the new seminary teacher. I was thrilled with the calling—for the first few weeks. Household organization, temple attendance, and housework suffered first. Then one of my children began exhibiting behavior that doctors said looked like a cross between high-functioning autism and bipolar disorder. Finally, my morning sickness pushed the whole family over the brink.

I had to acknowledge that despite my good intentions and priority sheet, I was out of balance again. I couldn't keep going, but I also didn't want to ask to be released. I cried a lot. I complained a lot. I prayed a little. Then I prayed some more. I read a compilation of BYU Women's Conference talks and happened upon Robert L. Millet's talk entitled, "After All We Can Do: The Meaning of Grace in Our Lives."

Brother Millet succinctly described my dilemma: "Instead of praying to know my limits, to know when my offering was acceptable, I prayed for more drive and more willpower."[2] How often had I prayed for more strength, more energy, or more efficiency? Had I asked amiss?

I contemplated my motivation and purpose. I studied the Topical Guide under "offering" and "acceptable." I prayed to know my limits and to know when my offering was acceptable. Eventually, I came to understand that giving only 30 percent of my time and talent to this particularly demanding calling was okay when the Lord said it was acceptable. The

Lord had called me knowing my limitations, and what I could offer was enough. He would provide what I could not.

The Lord's acceptance of my limited abilities brought my spirit knowledge of my worth as a child of God—knowledge my intellect had been unable to fully assimilate. Through the Spirit I knew that my willingness and desire to serve was the acceptable offering, not how much I achieved.

Reassurances of God's love came as I daily and weekly prayed to know the Lord's expectations. Sometimes the Lord's answer was, "Buck up! Put on a smile and just do it." At other times, the answer was, "Slow down. Do not try to 'steady the ark.' Others can accomplish this work. You need to focus on family or personal growth." And at still other times I was told, "Well done, thou good and faithful servant; enter into my rest."

Whatever the answer, I felt His love and knew that my acceptable offering was not my outward achievements. It was my commitment to serve the Lord cheerfully in whatever capacity He directed.

Each of us possesses different talents, abilities, challenges, and priorities. God created us to be unique. The Savior's injunction to "Judge not" (Matthew 7:1) resonated with added clarity as I recognized that only the Lord knows when an individual's offering is acceptable.

I was humbled by the thought that I have unrighteously judged another's 30 percent offering. I was humbled to realize that my perfectionism is another name for *pride.* I learned that only through my relationship with the Father can I obtain needed peace and self-acceptance.

Fast forward to another crazy Sunday. My husband supervises the baby—the youngest of five—in elders quorum. I'm presenting a Primary music lesson when my special-needs child starts to have a meltdown. With my Sunday smile pasted on my face, I try to finish the lesson. The perfectionist in me gets frustrated that she can't just pull it together for a few minutes to finish the lesson. *People will think I'm a bad parent. People will think my child is a spoiled brat.*

Then the Spirit reminds me of a few truths. It doesn't matter what "they" might unrighteously or ignorantly judge. It doesn't matter that I can't do the job 100 percent perfectly. What matters is my willingness and attitude. Heavenly Father reminds me that He knows and accepts my limited offering. This particular Sunday, I have to leave the Primary music lesson in other, capable hands. The Lord reminds me that patience and love for a challenging, special child is my offering for the day.

And it is enough.

Notes

1. "CHAOS" is a registered trademark of FlyLady and Company, Inc.
2. Robert L. Millet, in *May Christ Lift Thee Up: Talks from the 1998 Women's Conference* (Salt Lake City: Deseret Book, 1999), 60.

One Eternal Round

Lani B. Whitney

One eternal round
(you're tellin' me!),
no beginning and
no end.
Sameness
in this job of
day to day
mothering.
Eternal round of
messes today, eternal
round of joy forever—
Seen in smiles and
fat, up-stretched
arms
throughout these
days of preparation.

Strolling with Toddlers

Jennifer Boyack

When my son was two, we would occasionally walk his big sister to kindergarten. One day on the way home, I stopped to chat with a neighbor. My toddler screeched and twisted in the stroller, struggling to get out. Frustrated and wanting to have two minutes of adult conversation, I let him out. He bolted down a long stretch of grass directly toward a busy street, moving at top speed.

I ran, screaming, after him. No response. No slowing. Then, miraculously, he stopped abruptly at the curb. Winded and shaking, I picked him up. He grinned at me. I think I saw a glint in his eye.

My boy was incredibly curious, energetic, and swift—a dangerous combination. He was ambitious, too. Not only did he want to train to be a world-class sprinter, he also planned to be a great scientist and regularly conducted experiments in preparation, such as the one involving milk poured from a gallon container held perpendicular to the floor.

Hypothesis: If I pour this milk onto the floor and the distance from Mom is at least ten yards, her increase in velocity will be insufficient to stop me before the container completely empties.

Result: Hypothesis correct.

Like my little scientist, all seven of my toddlers have been challenging and lovable. Mothering them has made me acutely aware of my shortcomings and has stretched my heart. It has often brought me to my knees not only in wiping, scooping, mopping, and scrubbing, but in prayer and in pleading. And in complete exhaustion. Had I acted on all the frustrations of potty-training, my children would now be in foster care. I can't number the times I have kneeled to clean an unappealing mess. On tough days (read: *months*), I've often exclaimed, "I am *so* done with toddlers!"

One of the greatest frustrations is my nighttime nemesis— sleep deprivation. Many late nights I've wept, pleaded, and attempted absurd bargaining in exchange for a little rest. Some nights it seemed there was an invisible passing of the baton. Just as one child would settle back to sleep, another would awaken. I spent countless hours rigid in bed, too fearful to relax—knowing that if I got comfortable it would somehow trigger crying from the crib. How could they tell? They just could. It drained me of motivation and made me feel lazy. After particularly bad nights I sat like a zombie pining for naptime. My patience was worn and little accidents felt like huge disasters. Entry after entry in my journal begins, "I'm tired."

I knew the situation was serious when my fantasy of getting away for a night with my husband morphed into a desperate yearning to slumber for hours—or days—uninterrupted and alone.

But while I've had my fill of chaos, noise, and clutter, I've also had my share of cuddles, scribbled love notes, and unexpected *I love yous.* I think I've even learned a thing or two.

My mothering "experiments" have led me to discover a small miracle: although the frequency of difficult moments may appear to exceed pleasant ones, the depth of joy experienced can equal and exceed the depth of frustration. Thank heaven!

When our first child was about one-and-a-half, I first began to appreciate how heavily I would need to rely on patience, perseverance, and the power of repetition to survive the toddler years. We were living in my parents' home. My daughter loved their beautiful built-in bookshelves. Her favorite game, played several times daily, was pulling books off the shelf and letting them tumble to the floor. After each episode—trying to keep my cool—I kindly, but firmly told her, "The books belong on the shelf." Then I helped her to put them back in place. I was determined to teach my first child, young as she was, to be accountable for her actions.

One day after she emptied the bookshelf for probably the fifth time, I lost it. "Listen!" I yelled. "You are going to put every single book back on the shelf! EVERY ONE!"

My aunt stepped in from the garage right then and chimed, "This is when I would get out my camera and take a picture!"

I flushed red with mortification, sure I looked ridiculous taking that tone with a child less than two years old. But what about the first four times when I didn't get mad? Feeling defeated, I wasn't sure what to do. Removing the temptation didn't seem an option—it wasn't my home and the shelves were built-in. If I just cleaned the mess myself every time, what would she learn? How many times could we shelve the books together before she understood? Hoping I could last that long, I took a deep breath and handed my daughter a book to put back.

Sometime later, I sat with my back to the bookshelves and faced the wide French doors in front of me. Sun shone through the dozens of rectangular panes and painted a grid of shadows on the beige carpet. Enjoying the calm while my daughter played quietly outside, I closed my eyes and let the bright warmth sink in. Suddenly I heard her tender voice floating in through the screen as she sang, "I am a child of God and He has sent me here." She sang with such conviction. My heart swelled to aching.

Toddler adventures continued with "Dimples," our second. When he was two, his smile could stop complete strangers and compel them to sigh, "Awwww!" Many times, however, his behavior was less than adorable, and he didn't respond well to correction. When I tried to discipline him, he crumpled, consumed in whiny weeping—howling, really. I sometimes resorted to placing him in his crib until the tumult subsided. We would then talk about what had landed him there, but it wouldn't be long before we were reliving the same torment. I was stuck in a Dante-like world of déjà vu. My instinct was to be firm; don't tolerate misbehavior! But nothing I tried seemed to work.

Finally, my frustration tumbled out in prayer, and I pled desperately for help. "I don't know what to do. Please, please help me." One morning my son broke a rule and was beginning his typical disintegration.

This is it, I thought. *Be firm. Make him behave.*

And then came an unmistakable impression. *Hug him.*

I followed the impression, bridled my tongue, and kneeled to embrace him. He softened in my arms and hugged me back.

Not long after the milk incident with Mr. Scientist, he conducted another experiment: testing the strength of raw eggshells. He opened a full carton of eighteen eggs. Deftly, he grasped an egg and tapped it against another one with increasing pressure until he successfully found the amount of force necessary to crack both shells. To ensure the validity of his results, he repeated the experiment seven more times. At least he's thorough.

Even more difficult than his empirical antics was the fact that he refused to acknowledge my authority. As he ignored my commands, I got firmer and sterner until, finally, I spanked him.

He laughed.

What now? I wondered. *Spank harder?* I seethed, wanting to scream and cry. I couldn't go on like this.

Again, I kneeled and prayed. After pouring out my heart, the answer eventually came. *Praise him.* I tried it.

"Hey, honey, thank you for putting that away so quickly—you are awesome!"

"I love you!"

"You are such a good listener."

In just a few days, he started to respond, "Sure, Mom!" to my requests. He was even coming to me to share the good deeds he'd done. "Mom, I put all of my stuff away!" Other times he'd ask, "Can I help?" And my favorite change was how he would surprise me with fierce hugs and say, "I love you, Mom."

His experiments still continued—one day he tried peanut butter as a skin moisturizer and hair conditioner on his little brother—but when I had a reprimand on the tip of my tongue, he looked up without warning and uttered, "I love you, Mom. You're the best mommy."

Seven years have passed since the Scientist's dangerous dash from the stroller as a two-year-old. I still make the same walk every school day with my current—and quite possibly last—toddler. Over the past five months, we've marked our path with familiar stopping points (the stop sign, the yellow boat, the CURB!). For several weeks now, I've let my baby out of the stroller for the walk home. Instead of making life-threatening sprints toward the street, he knows how and where to stop and that he must hold on to the stroller when we cross the street. Today, for the first time, I let him walk both ways to school while I pushed an empty stroller.

As we went along, my neighbor commented, "You're not going to need that stroller much longer."

For an imperceptible instant, everything froze. Years of sleep deprivation, potty training, endless spills, messes, and accidents raced through my brain. I could even remember the words of my dear, wise mother-in-law saying, "You'll weep as you bear and raise them, and you'll weep when you're done."

Not me, I had begun to think. After years of feeling stretched to capacity and beyond, I was pretty sure I would feel at peace about it all—maybe even do a little jig. But suddenly, I feel like screaming again at my little toddler who is out of the stroller, "Stop! Stop!"

And the thought of packing away my stroller makes me want to cry.

The Catalogue Children

Heather Harris Bergevin

The Catalogue children
wear Dior suits, pressed,
and tulle-frilled dresses with patent on;
Mine roll downhill at church
in Sunday clothes and insist
on filling their good shoes
in the sandbox.

The Catalogue children
have a pirate ship, custom made
with organic, recovered teak, hand
carved
swords, on carbonized-bamboo flooring;
Mine make do
with a laundry hamper, cracked,
two mops, toilet paper tubes
and a beach sarong.

The Catalogue children
never get wet
or complain of mosquitoes
when photographed in fancy dress

at the evening party at the pier.
Mine fall in
while catching fireflies,
already-stained brown chocolate cake,
red punch, dirt, and lipstick kissed.

Catalogue children, let us come
play in your perfected
picture world.

Don't worry;
We will show you how.

Was Barbie from the Triassic Period?

Justine Clarice Dorton

Yesterday I watched my son and daughter playing together with each of their favorite toys. Barbie and Triceratops were happily frolicking through the den, apparently either married or dating. *Was Barbie from the Triassic period?* I wondered as the toys looked for some of Jocelyn's other Barbies (their offspring?). Once found, they were all picked up by a Pteranodon and flown through the house towards a volcano erupting in the kitchen. I crept around the house, trying without being noticed to see what Barbie and Triceratops's next adventure would be. After they climbed the volcano, they flew off (again on the Pteranodon) toward Barbie's summer home on the coast of Maine. How does a three-year-old girl understand the real estate market value of coastal property on the Atlantic?

What great kids I've got, I thought. *What a joy to have them in my home.* They were sharing, laughing, learning, and growing together. They took care of each other, meeting each other's needs, and finding ways to compromise for the benefit of both. It was a true "mom moment" where all the work comes together to make for one magical second.

These are my payoffs. These are what I work so hard for.

There's no money in parenting, in creating capable human beings, but these rewards tend to overwhelm my senses more than money ever could. I stand in the kitchen, listening to the giggles, wondering if we should have another baby.

Ten minutes later, party's over. Wailing, screaming, crying, hitting, time-outs—my *Little House on the Prairie* moment has come to a jarring halt. Gone is the feeling of accomplishment for raising such well-behaved children. Gone is the pride at hearing the words "please" and "thank you" uttered without persuasion. Gone is the idea of increasing the size of our family. In its place is that familiar knot in my stomach and blank look on my face. I re-enter my regular world—the one where I'm breaking up fights, fishing toothbrushes out of the toilet, and counting to ten to keep myself from yelling.

As the bellowing of children continues behind me, I walk back to the kitchen counter. I share a lot with the kitchen counter. It sees my smiles when I'm eavesdropping on happy children playing, and it often catches my tears as I spill frustrations onto the linoleum.

Am I having any success at being a parent? Am I building competent members of society, or am I grooming a batch of societal cast-offs?

Why on earth did the Lord think it would be a good idea to send some of his precious children to live in this house? He has, for unknown reasons, entrusted Don and me with these spirits. The job description is a mouthful: Raise them with an abiding testimony of the Lord. Teach them grace, charity, kindness, love, generosity, gratitude, leadership, humility, reverence, and faith. Oh, yeah, and along with all those things, teach them to read, to work, how to do arithmetic, algebra and geometry, how to take care of this world, to manage their resources, and above all, how to use the bathroom. And if you want strong, capable, thinking adults out of this deal, add about a thousand other things. So cover all those, too. Sometimes I cringe at the task in front of me. I retreat into my bedroom and pull up the covers, hoping to hide away from the overwhelming nature of motherhood.

Before I had children, my career was pressure-filled and demanding. I worked twelve-hour days and traveled to strange and exotic places. It was interesting, challenging and tremendously rewarding. No matter how difficult it got or how much stress I felt, it never felt like this. The demands from my children are exponentially more challenging.

In the workforce, I wasn't responsible for my colleagues' testimonies. I was never asked to teach a co-worker how to develop faith. Not once was I asked to clean up vomit at 2 A.M. Hindsight shows how easily I traveled through those years.

Instead I stand at the kitchen counter, listening to Barbie and Triceratops try to repair their relationship. *Can they do it?* I pin my hopes on their ability to reconcile their differences.

Have I taught them? Do they have the skills? Is this my performance review? Thoughts bounce around during their heated discussion.

It often feels as if evidence of my success or failure comes out in these moments—as if the true test of my parenting lies in their ability to exist without me. My goal is to succeed myself right out of a job. Some days that sounds pretty alluring. Other days, I ache with the knowledge that they won't need me forever. But today I wonder if I can pack their bags fast enough to get them on the next bus to Grandma's.

It occurs to me that Heavenly Father is a perfect parent. He does not take my imperfections upon Himself as a badge of bad parenting. He doesn't assume my flaws are due to some mistake on His part. Heavenly Father is creating me, shaping me, watching me struggle to get along, to meet others' needs. He's hoping, prodding, sending me to my room on occasion, trying to teach me to be more like Him. He's not hiding under the covers, wondering where He went wrong. He *knows* where I went wrong, but does not extend that reflection to himself. I, in turn, have my own set of hoping, prodding, and creating to do. Somehow, I've got to mourn my children's failures *with* them, not *for* them.

If Heavenly Father is the model for raising children and the expectation is perfection, why does He send us children in our youth? Why, in the midst of our own inexperience, does He carefully place children in our home, asking us to do what, for all practical purposes, is impossible?

Still staring at the kitchen counter, I've been lost in thought for several minutes. I notice the quiet, and awaken from my thoughts. It's not just in my head—peace has come back to the Dorton household. Barbie and Triceratops have worked it out. They're happily jaunting through the forest in the living room, looking for their baby eggs.

Is it just by chance that they found success? Has my influence been a part of anything that's happened in the last few minutes? Are there pieces of me somewhere inside them?

The answer has to be yes. Of course I'm in there. Of course I've had influence over them. But their success does not speak directly to my success, just as their failures do not always reflect mine.

Since Heavenly Father has purpose in all that he does, He *knows* that sending children into this home will not be a perfect experience. Maybe some of my children's success is from watching my failures. Sometimes I yell; sometimes I lose my temper; sometimes I speak without thinking. My children watch me do all these things.

Then they watch me fix it.

They watch me make amends, apologize, repent. They observe the ways in which I deal with conflict, both internal and external. They watch the Atonement play a part in my life. Maybe part of the purpose in sending children to imperfect homes is to teach them how to fix mistakes. Human nature seems hard-wired to make them, but it's those very mistakes that help us grow.

This *is* my performance review. But the real test is *not* how well my children behave. It's how I deal with these little people when I don't get the obedience and gratitude I expect from them. The Lord loves me with the same fervency whether or not I'm obedient and grateful. I, in turn, love my children, even as I'm pulling them off each other during a fight. I love them when they don't obey, don't listen, don't thank, don't flush. The Lord's words are echoed every day in my own. We're doing the same job—I as the apprentice—He as the Master.

I suppose the job involves all sorts of adult behavior. The list is quite a mouthful, things like patience, endurance, long-suffering, grace, kindness, love, charity, gratitude, forgiveness, leadership, reverence, faith—wait a minute, this list is starting to sound familiar.

At least I remember to flush.

That One in the Middle

Brooke Olsen Benton

Let me tell you about a boy. He was a little boy, but solid, heavy. His cheeks were magnificent, marshmallow things, perfect for nibbling on, and colored like peaches—rosy and soft. He was still a baby, too small to talk, his wails my only indication of whether he felt bereft in his crib, his smiles the sign of his joy.

This boy had auburn hair and eyes to match. He was a longed-for number two. He was a pain to deliver—all nine pounds, seven ounces of him—but an ecstasy to nurse and love. He won us over immediately with his abundant rolls of scented skin; and when he giggled, we sighed. How lucky for us to have such a happy baby!

But the coos were soon coupled with tears as he found his way to wariness. Near the pediatrician, at church, around any new faces, he clung to me with an urgency I'd never known. The way he held my fingers or my neck worried me even as I relished it. Still, he was *my baby,* and I was in love.

Let me tell you about a little boy who found trial in the title of "big boy" and, later, unexpected strength too.

My third pregnancy came sooner than expected. My body had just begun to lose its rounded heft; my head had just become reacquainted with my pillow for more than a few hours at a time. I was not ready to have another child, nor was my baby ready to be a big brother, which was clear from the amount of time he still spent on my lap, and in my arms. I could tell from the way we touched noses, from the yelling that ensued as he attended Nursery.

His life was still that of a baby's, full of long naps and pacifiers and the continual assurance from a blankie. But when he was twenty months old, I was already six months pregnant.

His wide shoulders and thick legs and utter babyness underscored a disparity I wasn't ready to deal with—the bittersweet reality that his one-year-old mind couldn't fathom, what my larger belly meant, what it would demand of him, and of me. He was already number two, already the product of a mother divided. He knew what it was like to be left to cry alone. He knew what hunger was and foraged for Cheerios freely. He learned patience in my lacking and waited as I helped his big sister first with things I couldn't do one-handed, like ponytails and hugs and art projects.

He never knew me in my eager, worried days. He never knew me unfettered and free, an entity only unto him—a lone planet to revolve around his sun. And that's what stung me most.

His eyes looked up at me, believing. They were my same

eyes, the shape of them, and just a few odd shades lighter than brown. They were eyes always trained upon his big sister, who dropped her baby brother once when she tried to carry him ("To help you, Mama."), leaving his eye bruised and welted, the purplish cast yellowing in places on his perfect skin.

His big sister was an only child till she was three. She was so different, so independent—the girl who, even as she started to walk, walked away from me. My brave girl began swim lessons as the dog days of August wilted into September, and she jumped into the endless aquamarine with abandon, unaware that she couldn't swim. During her lessons, my boy's eyes stayed glued to her even as he nestled deeper into my diminishing lap and his round paw of fingers clutched my arm. He sat at attention. He laughed at her.

With each successive lesson, he scooted farther away till one day he teetered on the edge of the pool and giggled as his feet touched the water that spilled into slippery puddles along the deck. The teacher pointed out his interest in the water. A week later I signed my boy (my baby!) up for lessons of his own.

Did I pause to consider what this would entail? I thought vaguely about the possibility of an empty lap for half an hour. I appreciated how I might feel cooler, how he might too, in the pool, sheltered from the waning sun, still strong with summer's intensity. And he could be a big kid like his sister. She loved it; he would too.

That first week, he screamed, clawing at his teacher as she reached out. As she drew him close, head submissive on her shoulder, he threw up on her. My boy was forced to swim after they squeezed fins onto his bulky feet—which were double wide and round and thick, feet that I had never been able to find shoes for, feet that had only walked barefoot—and put his face in the water.

What was my hurry?

His eyes were wide and brown as he came out of the water, cast with a look I never thought I'd see from one so little: complete resignation in my betrayal.

That he would love to swim later did not matter. He felt defeated, and I was brokenhearted at my hastiness. My boy splashed a little but gave up his attempts at escape. He didn't look for me on the deck, where I wrung the faded terry cloth of his small, hooded towel. My third baby, another girl, proved a proficient swimmer in my womb, and she kicked.

Now that my boy is three, strangers say he seems too tall to be a baby, too big to even just be three, but that he seems to still want to be a baby. I know what these comments must imply: a babyhood truncated, a middle child flanked by two dark-haired girls—similar in every way but age—that leave little room for him in-between, as they squish him and grab at his arms. They see a small, barrel-chested boy, who didn't choose his place right there in the middle, but stands there nonetheless, his brow creased and dissatisfied, his shoulders rounded. And I cringe that by virtue of being himself, wherever we are, he reveals what I fear in my heart: that there was never enough attention, never enough time. That he wasn't the baby long enough.

Last night we hurried through our brief goodnight kiss, and he lay down with a book. "I'll come read it to you in a few minutes," I told him. "Let me first get baby sister her bottle." I hurried from the room as he protested, and when I returned, he was sleeping, uncovered but holding fast to his blankie and his book.

As I retrieved his fallen duvet from the floor, I thought of how different he looked with his eyes closed, how placid and serene when I couldn't see his uncertain but beautiful eyes. Gone were the tears perpetually threatening to fall, the looks that questioned my devotion to him. Part of me longed to wake him, to read his book, fulfilling his solitary wish. But I didn't. Instead, I made sure his head was on the pillow and moved his legs, which were dangling off the side.

His elephant feet followed and I regarded them, so dirty. His feet are the road maps of his adventures—the true little boy. Dotted with rough calluses and marked by dozens of cracks, they're stained dark from over-exposure to dirt piles and from pushing trucks through the overgrowth of our backyard. They've been marinated in the outside elements and have the rough feel to prove it. These feet. These padded, pudgy feet—what a marvel. They often insist on running. Feet that wrinkle in the ocean, delighted; they withdraw, ticklish. They kick and they dance, and one time, they give an exaggerated leap off the side of the pool, only slightly slipping on the textured cement. And when my boy resurfaced triumphant, he turned to his sisters, who were watching, and they laughed, the three of them together.

He'll attend preschool this fall without knowing his ABCs, but he's already picked out a backpack. He builds Lego towers higher and higher, growing with his height. He longs to pedal a two-wheeler, to captain it on his own, but until then lets me push him. He yells at his sisters. As a middle child, he punches back, making a place for himself between them. He teaches me about tenderness, resilience, growth.

Let me tell you about him. He is my boy, and I am his mother.

Big Brother

Darlene Young

Propped,
bottom wedged firmly in the corner of the couch,
he sits with a blanket-wrapped bundle
posed precariously across his arms.
Mommy has so carefully coached him
he dare not move.
Muscles frozen lest he drop her precious package.

Mommy is home now
and she calls him her big boy
but he is still so small

so small

except his eyes large staring into the camera, caught
deer-like in oncoming headlights—
this tiny, squalling, sucking thing
in his arms, large as the future,
large as his world.

Tea Party Blessings

Heather Oman

I laughed when my husband, Nate, walked in from the store, five cucumbers in tow.

"I only need to make twenty-four bite-sized sandwiches," I told him. "How many cucumbers do you think I need?"

"Dunno." He shrugged as he dumped the vegetables on the counter.

I shook my head and started working on my food assignment. Two dozen cucumber sandwiches for the tea party that afternoon.

I'd never been to a tea party before. This one was in honor of our preschool administrator, who was leaving this year. The parents wanted to show their appreciation, so one mom decided we should have a tea. I had no idea what such a gathering would be like, but hey, if I didn't have to plan it, any kind of party was fine with me.

We arrived late for the party, having received bad directions to the house. The other mothers were already well into their food by then. I positioned my now rather limp white squares next to the rest of the finger food and filled a plate for my son and myself to share. He took off to play with the other kids from his class, and I sat down with the rest of the moms.

I knew some of the women from volunteering in the classroom. Others, however, I'd never met. One in particular, Angela, was unfamiliar to most of us, her son having joined the preschool late in the year. She introduced herself and we started the typical mom small-talk routine, chatting about being at home and comparing notes on our children. She asked the usual questions about how many children every-body had. To her surprise, all of us were mothers of an only child.

"I'm the only one with five children?" she said, incredulously.

From the other moms, I heard various murmurs of "Five! My goodness!" and "I don't know how you do it!"

I smiled and said, "You're the only one."

She smiled back and said, "Well, Heather, do you want more? Are you planning on having more?" And there it was.

The Question.

It's an innocent question, often asked by well-meaning people who aren't trying to pry. They're usually just trying to make conversation, trying to get to know me better. And usually, the person asking has no idea how much pain it invokes. I used to ask it myself. Not any more.

I thought about what to say to Angela. Our preschool

was affiliated with a Baptist ministry, and she was a member of the congregation. But how religious was she? I wondered how frank I could be with her, how much I could tell her about my struggles, my pleadings with the Lord, my many prayers that seemed to go unanswered. I decided to keep it brief.

"I'd love to have more," I answered. "But God hasn't blessed us with any more right now, so . . ." I ended with a small shrug.

Angela gave me a long look back and said, "God closes wombs, and He can open them. He opened Sarah's, and He can open yours. Is this the desire of your heart, to have more children? Then He'll open your womb, I promise. I pronounce that blessing upon you in the name of our Savior Jesus Christ, amen."

An awkward silence filled the table.

What exactly was the appropriate response to something like that?

I tried to play it light, and said, half laughing, "Are you a prophetess?"

She didn't laugh back. "No, but I am a servant of God, and you have a righteous desire to have children. God grants us the righteous desire of our hearts, according to our faith. You just need to build up your faith. I'm going to give you my e-mail address so you can tell me when you're pregnant.

Oh, I can't wait to get that message!" She got up, presumably to get something to write on.

I followed behind and in a low voice said, "You know, it's kind of complicated."

Complicated. That was the only word I could come up with. How else do you explain three years of disappointment and heartache to a woman who has just pronounced a blessing on you to have more children? What word in the English language can describe the anguish of miscarriage, of loss, of failed expectations?

I began to tell her about what I had suffered. She just waved it away and said, "Complicated for you, maybe, but not for God. He heals people all the time." She handed me her card. "Here's my address. Let me know when you're pregnant."

An e-mail. She was asking for an e-mail when I conceived, just as easily as if she were asking me to send a recipe or to set up a lunch date. I tucked her card in a little-used pocket of my purse, telling myself that I'd throw it away because the whole thing seemed ridiculous. Yet I didn't. I kept it, a tiny symbol of hope.

Over the next few weeks, I pondered her words. I'd called the situation complicated. She'd told me that it was simple, that God would bless me, if I only had faith. It was true that the last three years had been faith-shaking. I'd gone through four miscarriages, infertility treatments, and, most recently, a diagnosis of polycystic kidney disease (PKD).

We'd been blessed with a son early in our marriage and had hoped for a big family, but with each trial, our chances of bringing more children into the world slipped farther and farther away. In light of my PKD, a condition worsened by pregnancy, bearing another child seemed all but impossible.

I thought about what it meant to build up my faith, but wondered, *What more can I do?* I'd tapped every resource Western medicine had to offer. I'd even explored Eastern medicine and a variety of alternative healing methods. All of that was interesting, but ultimately frustrating. I prayed harder and longer for an answer about my miscarriages than I had prayed for anything in my life. So many times I had asked the Lord for another child that my words felt like vain repetitions. All of my expectations about my future, the choices that I felt were mine to make, seemed to be stripped from me, and I found myself floundering in uncertainty. I wanted clarity, answers, anything, from anywhere. I got nothing.

Regardless of pain and suffering, life has a way of moving on. Nate got a new job in a new city, and we prepared to move our small family. I pushed the tea party blessing and my pregnancy woes to the back of my mind as we made the transition from a big city to a small town, from a small townhouse to a house with a yard and fence. I got happily entrenched in tilling a garden, setting up house, building our home.

I was also forced to focus on the issues with my kidneys. I did research on PKD, trying to gather all the information possible about my new diagnosis and what it meant for me and my family. I learned that in as little as ten years, I could need dialysis and a kidney transplant. This knowledge fundamentally changed the way I viewed my body. Admittedly, I was scared. The thought of a kidney transplant or a life on dialysis genuinely frightened me.

My prayers stopped being vain repetitions as I prayed about my new fears. I also began to feel profound gratitude about what my body could still do. It was still whole. I could still run, swim, play games with my son. I had no idea how long that would last. I stopped banging the gates of heaven, asking for more, and instead starting asking to simply keep what I had. Little by little, peace made its way back into my heart as I humbled myself, poured out my gratitude, and prayed to the Lord to help me cope with this trial.

Gradually, my relationship with God changed. As I came to realize that faith is connected with gratitude and humility, I also considered the possibility that the Lord *was* in a position to bless me, that He had always been in a position to bless me. I just had to accept what He offered. Angela was right. God would bless me, if only I had faith. Maybe I wouldn't get a baby, but I became aware of other blessings in my life that came as I drew closer to the Lord. I was blessed with inner strength, peace, a renewal of spirit, and a lightness of heart I hadn't experienced for a long time. It was a relief to feel like I was communicating with God again, to feel that my prayers were being heard.

We settled into our new life and decided that we should start the adoption process, something we'd talked about before. But it had always been our last resort. We also wanted to be in a more permanent living situation before we considered it, without a possible move on the horizon. Nate's new job gave us that permanence, and we felt that we were now ready to pursue adoption. With that decision came more peace, more relief, as if a burden had been lifted from my body.

I was giving the situation entirely to God now. I felt I was finally humble enough to say, "Thy will be done." No more tests, no more poking, no more failed hypotheses about what was wrong. It was over. I could rest.

One day as I cleaned out my purse, I came across Angela's card, and her blessing came rushing back. I smiled and tucked the card back into the pocket. *I'll e-mail her when we adopt,* I thought. *That will make her happy.* I went about my life, feeling at last that I'd moved on, past the pain of all of my failed pregnancies.

Then came the heartburn.

I was helping a friend who was on bed rest when suddenly, I felt I needed some of her Tums. Like many other pregnant women, she had them by her side at all times, and I asked her for some. She gave me a funny look and said, "Are you pregnant too?"

I said, "I don't get pregnant, remember? It must have been the pizza we had earlier." What I didn't tell her was that I had never suffered from heartburn in my entire life . . . *except* when I was pregnant.

Although Nate and I had decided we were going to adopt, we hadn't tried to prevent a pregnancy, either. When I got home that night, I dug out an old pregnancy test. I told myself it was probably nothing, to not get my hopes up, that perhaps it really was the pizza. I hadn't even missed my period yet. But I wanted to make sure.

Two pink lines. Two. Immediately. I was pregnant. Pregnant, four and a half years after my first child was born. Pregnant, two years after my last miscarriage. Pregnant, nine months after my diagnosis of PKD. And pregnant, just three months after a woman who was a stranger pronounced a blessing on me that I'd have more children, according to the desire of my heart.

That heart began to pound as I carried the test to my husband. He blinked at it, and we looked at each other. He smiled and professed his happiness, but I knew what we were both thinking.

Are we ready for this? Are we ready for another disappointment? Are we ready for it to work out this time? What about my PKD?

We'd been told that the risks of a pregnancy with PKD could be huge. It seemed a miracle that we were pregnant, but we both knew we might need yet another miracle: strength to handle whatever happened next.

I hid my pregnancy from everybody as long as I could. I couldn't bear the thought of explaining things if we lost this one, too. At first, I felt nervous and anxious all the time, wondering if and when another miscarriage would occur. I made up excuses about why I couldn't run with my friends any more, why I couldn't go to church. When I did go, I locked myself in the kitchen and threw up into the sink to avoid meeting somebody in the bathroom and having to answer awkward questions. I prayed constantly that we'd keep this baby, but this time I also prayed that I could accept the outcome, whatever it was.

At the advice of my primary care doctor, I sought out a perinatologist who had experience with pregnancy and PKD. I trekked out to see her almost every week. She prepared me for a rough time and put me on bed rest. At thirteen weeks, when she couldn't find a heartbeat with the magic microphone wand on my belly, my heart dropped, sure that my fears were confirmed. She turned on the ultrasound machine, and we saw the unmistakable moving blip of a heartbeat on the screen. That tiny blip gave me hope, and I began to really believe that this time things would be okay.

That feeling of peace grew each week. That is not to say that the pregnancy was easy. I was, after all, considered a complicated patient, and I often relied on the skill and experience of my doctor to keep me and the baby healthy. But even though she insisted that my baby would most likely be an early arrival, perhaps accompanied by a NICU stay, I continued to feel calm, knowing that whatever happened, we'd rely on the Lord to help us through it. He'd brought us so far already.

Imagine our joy when our daughter showed up at thirty-nine and a half weeks, eight pounds, two ounces, after eighteen hours of labor but just one push. A rather simple delivery.

"She's here," I whispered, as the doctor handed her to me. "She's finally here." I couldn't stop the tears flowing down my face as I wiped her little body with a towel. I cleaned her face, ears, arms, legs, and tiny toes. "She's perfect," I said, as I brought her to my breast. My doctor let me try to nurse her before she took the baby to be measured and weighed.

"Hello, my little miracle baby," the doctor said.

Yes, our miracle baby. We named her Elizabeth. Some say the name means *God's oath.* Others say it means *one anointed by*

God, or *one dedicated to God.* We figured all of those meanings were appropriate for our new little girl.

I e-mailed Angela and told her of our joyous news. She never responded. I still don't know what to make of the blessing she gave me that day, a year before my daughter was born. Whatever her intentions, her words of encouragement came at a time when I desperately needed them, and I'll always be grateful to her for that.

A few days after we brought Elizabeth home, I felt a familiar pain in my side. My kidneys were shifting back from their displaced position in my abdomen. The pain was a reminder that I'd need to go back to my kidney specialist soon to determine the extent of the damage done by the pregnancy. It was a reminder that my struggles with my body weren't over, and indeed might never be. I still faced all of the same problems as before Elizabeth was born. The Lord had seen fit to bless us with a second child, but my body was still far from healed.

Yet the fear about my body was no longer there. The discouragement and frustration I'd lived with for so long were gone. My faith was finally stronger, which meant that I knew in whom I trusted. I knew that despite the physical difficulties that most certainly lay ahead, I could face my future with hope. God would bless me in His own time, in His own way.

"See?" I'm sure Angela would say. "Simple."

The Measure of a Mother

Kylie Turley

When I was young, I wanted the neighbor's cream-of-something-soup casserole with its side of iceberg-salad-in-a-bag. Their unerringly straight slices of store-bought white bread seemed nearly celestial. But such memories have long-since faded behind those of home-grown produce and home-made desserts.

I grew up assuming that all moms regularly served scrambled eggs, buttermilk biscuits, and sliced honeydew melon for breakfast at 7 A.M., that other mothers also dished out from-scratch macaroni and cheese for lunch, and "threw together" a dinner of cheese-topped garden vegetables, strawberries in vanilla cream, corn-on-the-cob, and Bul Kogi for dinner. At the time, I arrived at the table happy to eat, vaguely grateful, and insensitively oblivious to how all these masterpieces were whipped up.

I "helped" by making cookies. I can still hear my mom calling to me when I was eleven, "One cup sugar, one cup brown sugar," as she walked down the green and yellow linoleum stairs to the basement. I measured and dumped. Up she came, arms loaded with jars of applesauce produced from the tart apples grown during the short Wyoming season. "One cup butter, then mix." She put the jars on the counter and turned toward the laundry room, having heard the loud buzz of the dryer cycle shutting down.

I waited, lost. The rest of the recipe was a jumble of eggs, flour, salt, baking soda (or baking powder?), vanilla, and chocolate chips. I couldn't move forward a teaspoon without her, though I took full credit for the cookies in the end.

After my own children began to outgrow rice cereal and jars of smoothly pureed vegetables, I wanted to cook my mother's food, to feed the little mouths who depended on me something other than greasy French fries and bone-depleting soda pop. I hunted down my mom's recipes and found faded index cards with typed-up lists of ingredients—but no directions. None of the "cream butter and sugar for 3 minutes on high" Betty Crocker-type stuff. Nothing. Moreover, the ingredients often lacked measurements. "Vanilla" was always standing naked and alone, something to pour or drip according to taste.

I swallowed hard and felt a scatter of goose bumps rise on my arms. It was nothing to get upset about, I told myself, but I couldn't stop scanning cards faster and faster, suddenly feeling panicked. How was I to cook like Mom without precise guidelines? These recipes were lists, not instructions; common principles without step-by-step tutoring. I wanted results. Guarantees. Success.

I salvaged a few cards that had clear-cut directions, no doubt given to her by other people. A few weeks later, I meticulously followed the recipe for Bul Kogi, marinating the meat twenty-four hours in a Ziploc bag while I dreamed of the spicy Korean taste I remembered from my youth. The next night I organized dinner, barbequed the meat, and insisted that everyone be seated and waiting when I brought out the food. I dished out three kids' plates and sat down. I returned to the fridge for butter (someone didn't want soy sauce on his rice) and a different kind of salad dressing ("white ranch" was suddenly unacceptable), annoyed that things were not going the way I'd planned.

Finally my turn came: I tasted. And flinched.

With my whole family still around the dinner table, I called my mother long distance. The kids kept eating, eyeing me and chewing with interest while I demanded to know where I went wrong.

"Oh," Mom said, "I like to add a bit more sesame oil," followed by, "I never put that much pepper in," and, "I don't know—I just dump until it looks right," and finally, "Did you cut the meat in the right direction? It's tougher if you cut it wrong."

The dinner was fine, really, but it didn't taste like I remembered. Apparently there is no recipe that re-creates my memory of home and my mother's cooking. Even though

I had planned methodically, my organization and precision were all for naught.

Ironically, I still feel a hypnotic pull toward precise measuring and meticulous directions. Despite discovering that even the most precise of recipes will not guarantee the results I want, I'm a zealous measurer in too many aspects of my life. I measure my time, my talents, my righteousness. I measure my tummy when I'm pregnant and my dress size when I'm not. I measure how long my kids watch TV and the amount of money in my bank account. I measure sentence lengths when I edit papers, and I measure words and emotions when I'm worried about relationships. I measure how much food my two-year-old throws on the floor, how much better I'll feel if I hit the snooze button one more time. I measure the miles I drive and the length of the vacuum cord. I have speedometers, pedometers, rulers, scales, and measuring tapes.

I know how to measure.

But does rigid measuring guarantee success? Do I cling to the safety of tools rather than allowing for nuance, openness, and possible failure? Do I fully understand the complexities of the people, children, situations, and relationships that I'm measuring?

A few years ago, I had a crisis of faith. I was pregnant and anemic, with a temper-tantrum-throwing baby and a chronically busy, workaholic, bishopric-serving husband. I taught English part-time and was Young Women's president, no small job in my "inner city Provo" ward. For months I felt myself depleting like a balloon with a small pinprick. I waned, I faded—shrinking in spirit and determination. Arriving home from church one Sunday, I shifted the car to park, turned off the ignition, and rested my forehead on the steering wheel, contemplating the twenty-step walk to the front door. Too far, it seemed. Just too far. Especially when it included a heavy diaper bag slung over my shoulder, scriptures cradled in one arm and a hot, sleeping baby in the other. I could not make it.

I would have cried, but I was too exhausted for tears. So I just sat. For ten, twenty, thirty minutes, I rested while my child slept with her neck kinked sideways in her car seat. Finally I heaved my pregnant body out of the car and hauled everything inside, blaming my fatigue on a lack of faith and wondering why God left me comfortless when I was trying so hard.

My husband gave me a blessing. Heavenly Father apparently wanted to tell me that I was mistaken: during this whole ordeal when I thought my faith was evaporating, I was, to quote the blessing, "gaining in faith."

The words rang true, even though I still haven't figured out exactly what He meant. All I know is that my measuring stick was exactly 180 degrees off, completely backwards and inside out.

I say I lost faith. He says I gained.

He measured me in an incomprehensible way and found me whole, good, faithful, growing. That thought lifts and mystifies me. It is stunning to learn that I do not know how to measure, not even to measure myself.

Looking back, it is obvious that I should have learned about measuring years ago. Culinary creativity nudged me in the right direction: feeding my family three meals a day for years, noting individuals' likes and dislikes, getting bored with tried-and-true basics, remembering my mom's effort-less dash-of-this and pinch-of-that method of cooking—all these things had much to teach me.

It dawned on me that I had turned a momentous corner when my newly married sister phoned from Idaho asking, "How do you make applesauce? I called Mom, but all she said was to put in 'some' water and cook it for 'a while.'"

I stalled, asking about her husband and her work. I knew she was looking for the same things I had: amounts, precise directions, numbers and times, which is why I had to pull out my red-and-white-checked *Better Homes and Gardens* cookbook to help her.

I haven't looked at the recipe for years; these days I just fill up my big silver pot with apples, put in water about halfway up, then cook the stuff until the mix gets mushy. I add "some" sugar—how much depends on the type of apples I found on sale, my annual quirky desire for sweetness, and whether I have a baby who should be eating "no added sweeteners" applesauce. And there you have my recipe. There are ingredients (apples and water) and measurements ("fill" the pot with apples, "halfway" with water). It's vague, I admit—but very adaptable.

Which is precisely why I love "fruit drink." In twenty years, when my children come searching my files for the fruit drink recipe, they won't find an old index card; fruit drink has no recipe because there *is* no recipe. But it's easy: simply throw any fruit that is about to go bad into a big Ziploc bag and keep it in the freezer. When the bag gets full, dump it into the blender, pour in a can of Sprite, some ice cubes, and some water. Blend it smooth (or chunky—it really doesn't matter). Or if you want to make it for breakfast, nix the Sprite and use milk instead. Add sugar if you want. It almost always turns out, and I name it according to what happened to go in: banana-strawberry; peach-kiwi-cantaloupe; berry delight. Sometimes I call it "Tutti Frutti," a tricky name that inspires even my middle child to drink it no matter what happens to be blended in. Fruit drink is malleable and healthy, created from whatever fruit is available and a few basic ingredients (i.e. water and ice cubes).

In cooking, I have become my mother. My memory contends that my disasters are more frequent and my eaters more picky, but despite the whines ("How many bi-ites do I ha-ave to eat?"), I can no longer force myself to follow a disaster-proof, direction-laden, measurement-precise recipe. I am no longer the type who buys into the convenient straight-from-the-box mentality.

A summer night calls for a light marinara, full of barely blanched vegetables, chunky tomatoes, and some Italian spices, while a winter evening needs a thick, heavy spaghetti sauce—both can be made from the same ingredients, but tweaked for the occasions, the individual tastes, even the weather.

What I am slowly realizing is that motherhood is more like marinara than I ever imagined. The "righteousness recipe" I originally had in mind is rigid and unworkable. Precise directions for celestial mothering call for effortless glorying in little baby fingers and toes, smiling at the joyous antics of toddlers, listening (seriously) to the ramblings of pre-teens, and whipping up healthy and wholesome meals.

But there are hard days when I look around my home and cringe at the ingredients: children whining about the "green things" in dinner, a baby splattering cooked carrots, a husband still at work, three reading charts to sign and return, a Gospel Doctrine lesson to prepare, and a migraine hammering in my left temple. I feel myself creating a home-cooked disaster. The "righteousness recipe" might as well be pureed to pulp with the fruit drink. I choose to lose my temper, spitting sharp commands and spreading irritation.

On those days, I go to bed devastated. I kneel and pray that my cup of frustration and tablespoon of anger will ruin only dinner, not my children or my eternal efforts. I beg to be filled, so that I, in turn, can pour out love and time, stir in kindness and forgiveness, and fold together a dash of discipline—all according to individual tastes and needs. I know God has a different way of measuring. I know He can use any ingredients and turn them to good. I pray that He is somehow creating a masterpiece of me, even when I don't follow the directions and even when I haphazardly change the ingredients.

These ideas roll around in my head and make me think of measuring, creating, and my mother. She bakes love so it wafts and floats through the air like rich and gooey chocolate-chip cookies. Her dinner is flexible enough to feed two or twenty, and, no matter what boils on the stove, she can look me in the eyes and talk about what matters, sprinkling the discussion with salty wisdom. Her dinners never taste the same, because she uses whatever is on hand, what's fresh, what's growing—and then adapts accordingly.

She insists that she's not creative and that she "needs to

be better." Perhaps she's right, if we measure on someone's rigid and exacting checklist of righteousness.

But I don't really think so. As far as I'm concerned, my mother has learned something more important: she knows how *not* to measure. She changes every recipe, and, inevitably, she changes the taste of everything she creates—usually discovering in the process that the changes were just what was called for today, for this child, for this challenge.

She probably doesn't realize that her imaginative cooking has taught me of God, His work, and my work as a mother: the grace of *not* measuring is exactly the right ingredient.

Inheritance

Darlene Young

I got your jewelry, a couple of scarves and an old dress
I claimed just because it looked like you.

But familiar though the earrings are, the scarf, the dress,
the emerald pin, no matter how I squint into the past
I can't make out your face and now I fear
I never really saw it. Being a mother too,
this worries me.

But also when you died I got your books
and, reading them, I find you after all.
Your voice, your voice, with sweetest clarity,
rings through the words you chose to share with me.

And so in fear of leaving my kids motherless—
and as a feeble recompense for all the times
I sneak into their rooms at night
to beg forgiveness from their twitching eyelids
for the petty strictness of my ways—
the one thing I make sure of all my days
is that they get my voice.

Stories they will build their worlds on, stories
teaching how to yearn, tales that break
their hearts apart then knit them back
a little softer—all the words I got from you.

Your voice in mine will carry on
in their bright dreams after I'm gone.

Going Up the Mountain

Allyson Smith

I stand at the back of a Boeing 747 with my five-year-old daughter, who is dancing the jitterbug with her legs crossed. A middle-aged businessman who reached the back of the airplane at the exact nanosecond we did has been edging closer and closer to the "in use" toilet cubicle. When the door finally (finally) folds open, the man darts in front of my advancing daughter, wedges himself inside, and shuts the door with a swoosh. We stand there, my daughter and I, plastered against the wall while the airline attendants pry drinks and snacks from around us and the line for the bathroom builds to one side. The claustrophobia without is beginning to reflect the claustrophobia and tension within. I feel compressed to the point of implosion.

It is early summer, ten days in at most, and we're flying west. The winter was long and frigid, our apartment dark and tight, and somehow our town managed to skip spring entirely. We went from snow at the beginning of May to hundred-degree temperatures by the end. One of my religion teachers used to say, "Everyone needs their personal Sacred Grove." I can see where he's coming from, but I haven't even had my own personal bathroom time for years. Where am I supposed to find a sacred grove?

I've kept sane the past three months by envisioning a trip west, full of nothing but space and silence. What I really want is to live in a cabin so far out in the mountains they would have to airlift toilet paper to me. I've always equated peace with altitude; the mountains are where I go to regroup. But this kind of altitude, in an airplane wedged next to this kind of "cabin," is not what I need.

Three more minutes, and the man has not emerged. For the first time in my life I seriously consider picking the bathroom lock on a stranger.

* * *

When I was younger, I envisioned myself living in some cabin on a mountainside overrun by quaking aspen and pine. I would have a dog, and a couple of horses. As I grew older and started dating Bryan, he made his way into the vision as well. In my mind, we took long walks, listening to the wind in the trees and the rocks rattle and slide under our feet. It was always quiet on that mountainside; I could think or read a lot. I don't remember ever yelling or getting frustrated at that imaginary cabin. And I certainly don't remember someone shutting the bathroom door in my face (the cabin had indoor plumbing) every time I needed to take care of business.

What I loved most about the idea of that cabin was the thickness of the silence; not a silence devoid of *sound,* but one devoid of *noise.* The kind of silence you can almost hold in your hand. It was the same silence I felt every time I went up the real mountains—the Wasatch range—behind the home where I grew up. And I went up often.

There is something about the mountains that funnels the Spirit like it funnels the wind and the snow. In the crook of the canyon or topping out on the peak, even winding through the aspen on the lower slopes, the Spirit can hit with such force it can knock you off your feet. At least that's how it felt to me. I would sometimes take my scriptures with me and read about Moses and Abraham and Nephi and the brother of Jared going up the mountain when they needed revelation. I thoroughly understood why. Many of my most poignant spiritual experiences barreled into me on those slopes.

I understood, I think, to the point of using the mountains as a crutch. Whenever I felt overloaded or uninspired, I just changed my scenery. Eventually I forgot how to regroup without mountains or deserts or some other spectacularly desolate landscape to give me enough depth perception to look upward rather than outward or inward. At some point I lost the ability to close my eyes and breathe in the perspective on my own.

* * *

A few years ago, Bryan and I moved eastward from the Wasatch front, but not far enough east for the landscape to climb; we moved to the middle of the Midwestern plains. I knew I'd miss the mountains, but I was surprised to find how absolutely naked I felt without them. How unhinged. After a year in Indiana we drove back to Utah for a visit, but the rejuvenation from a handful of hikes didn't last long. It's been two years since our last trip, and I've been in desperate need of some sustainable redirection. So we plan another trip west, and consider our travel options: car or airplane.

The last time Bryan and I flew with the kids, our sons were two years old and four months old, and we were moving home from France. The four of us, with all our luggage, caught the early-morning train to the Paris airport. Unfortunately, our diaper bag did not make it. Over the years, the trauma of that ensuing twenty-four-hour voyage—without snacks, blankies, pacifiers, or diapers—was potent enough to keep us from hauling our expanding family onto another airplane; at least with a car you can always stop and get out. But this time, eager to arrive at our destination, we bought plane tickets for the whole family. The three older kids packed books, games, snacks, toys—anything we could think of to help pass the time—into their own backpacks to access at will. I thought we were in for a smooth ride; this was, after all, only a three-hour flight.

Things began well. The boys, who have no memory of that other plane ride, were ecstatic. They wanted to know all about lift and thrust, seating arrangements, and especially the "free drinks cart." Within fifteen minutes of take-off however, the plane hit cruising altitude, the novelty wore off, and the seat-belt sign was still on. Due to some minor turbulence, the sign stayed on for most of the flight, and the drink cart didn't leave its docking port for over an hour. No one wanted to read. Fights broke out over game rules, the two-year-old kept bolting down the aisle, and the baby spit up on my shirt.

Somehow, the six seats filled with our family had warped back home, and Bryan and I were being bombarded with all of the usual complaints and irritants. Only three hours, indeed. *Fifteen minutes down,* I thought to myself as things began to unravel. *Two hours and forty-five minutes to go.*

* * *

After my daughter's record-breaking potty-hold, I find myself back in my seat, feeling anything but calm. This flight is turning out to be intensely more grating. I stare out the window, thinking about my cabin in the woods and some dense quiet.

The irony is killing me: after three years on the flatlands, pining for mountains to calm and redirect me, I find myself at thirty-five thousand feet—roughly the height of Mount

Everest—frothing with frustration. *Maybe altitude isn't the key,* I think. *Maybe it's just silence. I need to get some of that.*

* * *

We don't have much of silence in our apartment, with its cinderblock walls and thin-carpet-over-cement floors. In this complex, once you have three children you can move into a double apartment, "double" being literal: maintenance crews knocked out a doorway between the smaller bedrooms of two back-to-back apartments, creating a horseshoe layout with exterior doors on each end. Our five children sleep in the "hallway" created by the connected bedrooms, their bunk beds and dressers shoved against the outside wall. Every room flows into another room; not even the bathroom is insulated against the cacophony. So when my lava starts to boil, I either erupt or leave. In a perfect world, I would always leave. Somewhere. Anywhere.

But my world is not perfect, and there are times (I'm not proud to admit) that I am too far gone to get myself out the door. If I'm lucky, Bryan is home, and he sends me off to a "mountain" at the library or the lake or the museum downtown. He's been sending me more and more of late, and I am starting to feel like a siphon or a drug addict; I need more and more solitude to pull back up to functional.

He kept the kids at home all last week while I spent three days in Chicago with my nine-month-old daughter and my infant nephew, ostensibly babysitting for my sister who was attending a conference, but in reality babysitting myself. Based in a quiet hotel room, without a house to clean or homework to help with, caring for two infants felt very nearly like doing nothing. I went on long walks; I did a lot of reading. There were no mountains in sight, yet I felt the resignation and frustration receding at high speed.

But here's the bizarre part. It took me two days to get my sanity back; by the end of the third day I was bored. Honestly. The silence was becoming oppressive. When I headed off to catch the train home, I was actually eager to get back to the sounds of exuberance and aggravation that reverberate through our place like the front row at a Rolling Stones' concert. The break had pulled me out of a dark hole, but I was not sure if it had managed to refill it.

And teetering on the edge of a dark hole isn't all that much better than being down in one. *Is it?*

* * *

Minor turbulence turns major as we break back through the clouds. The baby is asleep in my arms, and the boys are reading in absolute silence on either side of me. Sweet silence. They calmed down after they got some soda—counterintuitive as that may be—and I have had a full fifteen minutes to relax into my seat, with the sleep-heavy baby's wet breath on my chest. The sky outside above the white horizon is so starkly, blankly blue that it looks like no weather at all. So blue on blue on blue, in fact, that I am having trouble looking at it. Jolting back through the clouds feels good, even if it does wake the baby.

I am frustrated by the motion, but I miss it when it goes, just like I miss the pandemonium of our family when I am away. Maybe I wasn't meant to be a hermit after all. Silence and mountains are good conduits for me to access the Spirit—and some sanity—but I'm finding that they aren't the only routes, and certainly not the most lasting ones. Real fulfillment, real spiritual feasting, is internal after all. I just need to find a consistent way to get above the smog line when I'm overwhelmed. I mean, if I can learn to get a deeper sense of the Atonement while praying in a car loaded with kids, or while reading my scriptures with the theme song from *Gilligan's Island* reverberating in the background, then maybe I won't need a literal mountain so much. Maybe I'll be able to climb heavenward within myself.

I do need silence and a change of scenery in good, big doses from time to time, and I'll take the mountains whenever I can get them. In the meantime I'll try learning how to close my eyes in the middle of the playroom and redirect myself heavenward.

So if we're talking one day and you see my eyes cross lazily and a pleasant, relaxed expression roll onto my face, don't be alarmed. I've just gone up the mountain.

I'll come back down for some chaos soon.

East of the Sun, West of the Moon

Melonie Cannon

Motherhood, a winter-white
    bear,
taps on the cold window
of my sleep
and asks for me.

I bow to the shivering moon
and climb,
still warm and heavy from my bed
onto its back,
clinging to the white fur
as slippery as a million miniscule
    icicles.

We lumber through days, bleary-
    eyed,
inseparable,
always plodding forward, hip to
    hip,
returning to each sleepless night,
and the fixed unchanging ritual.

The bear burrows under the
    covers,
breathing hard and rich,
warming the hibernating air
that surrounds us as we lie
side by side
like indifferent lovers
waiting for the first light to ache
the room into being.

I wonder to the dark
About the beast that rests beside
    me,

If I had a tiny tallow—
with a wick like a mighty burn-
    ing sun—
that flicker of light
might illuminate the bear's
    beauty.
I could see what I've
wrapped myself around.

Or with three burning drops
of melted wax, I would wake
Motherhood, startling it,
rousing it in a roar
of betrayal and confusion,
sending it back to the frigid
    forest
so I could sleep
alone.

Instead, we are caught together
in a blush of mid-light,
trapped, partners in a staggering
    dance,
East of the sun and
West of the moon.

Wonder Mold Mother

Lisa Hardman

Woman's life today is tending more and more toward . . .
"Zerrissenheit"—torn to pieces-hood. She cannot live perpetually in
"Zerrissenheit." She will be shattered into a thousand pieces.
—Anne Morrow Lindbergh, Gift from the Sea

My daughter's fifth birthday party was nearly over when I noticed the remains of her Princess Barbie birthday cake. Deep gouges, carved by the greedy fingers of my daughters and nieces, crisscrossed the lavender frosting, revealing the chocolate cake skirt underneath. Every sugary-pink flower was gone. One of my younger nieces had innocently licked the sweet frosting off of the plastic doll pick: a bare-breasted, half-Barbie with a pointy stem instead of legs extending from the base of her torso.

Disconnected from her cake skirt, the doll pick lay discarded on the serving plate, exposed and vulnerable. As a final, dishonoring act, one of the girls had callously removed the arms from the doll's torso and stuck them into the cake skirt. The result was a freakish representation of the female body, a surreal piece of artwork of which even Salvador Dali would have approved.

I thought back to the moment when my daughter looked at me with those trusting brown eyes and asked for a princess birthday cake. I knew next to nothing about cake decorating, but how could I say no? She believed that I was capable of creating magic. I wanted to believe it too. Caught up in her unquestioning faith, I went to the craft store for cake-decorating supplies, wondering why it was always up to me to orchestrate celebrations. Though I wanted to wilt under my overwhelming feelings of inadequacy, I plastered a smile on my face for her sake and pretended to know what I was doing.

My compulsion to provide the perfect cake overtook all rational thought. The evening before the party, I stayed up past midnight to bake the cake skirt in a special Classic Wonder Mold pan. Early the next morning, I rolled up my sleeves, took a deep breath, and began the task of adorning the cake with a loaded frosting bag. After an hour of extruding hundreds of pink frosting flowers onto wax paper, I shook the cramps out of my aching hand, stepped back, and surveyed the pristine, immaculate rows. A quick glance at the clock revealed that time was running out. I worked quickly to frost the cake skirt and doll's torso.

Why didn't I just buy a princess cake? I wondered. *Why am I pressuring myself to be super mom again? Who really cares about all this effort? What am I trying to prove, anyway?*

Minutes before the guests arrived, my daughter skipped

into the kitchen and lurched to a stop in front of the finished cake.

Her eyes opened wide. "Oh, Momma! She's the prettiest princess *ever!*" She threw her little arms around my waist, then ran off to meet her cousins at the door.

The cost of the past forty-eight tedious and stress-laden hours was suddenly forgotten. My frazzled nerves, frayed emotions, and throbbing head had been laid on the altar to give my daughter the "happy" in "happy birthday," and she was pleased.

* * *

In spite of the party's success, the image of the marred princess cake continues to haunt me. Days, weeks, and even months later, the pathetic, bizarre figure works its way into my psyche. Birthday cakes are meant to be eaten and enjoyed. So why am I so troubled about its demise?

"Woman instinctively wants to give," says Anne Morrow Lindbergh, "yet resents giving herself in small pieces . . . giving herself purposelessly. What we fear is not so much that our energy may be leaking away through small outlets as that it may be going 'down the drain.'" Painstakingly, lovingly, I had poured myself wholeheartedly into creating something magical, and it was obliterated in ten minutes.

I don't want to admit that, after thirteen years of dedicated motherhood, *I* am the mangled cake incarnate, disjointed and stripped of distinctiveness. I have given myself away, piece by piece, until my personality, my individuality, and my uniqueness have become obscured behind diapers, laundry, and meal preparation. Some days, in the midst of raising four children, I feel like nothing more than a live-in servant, a human Kleenex, a biddable genie whose own dreams and wishes are set aside time and time again.

Even as I make the effort to do something for myself, to build and mold myself into a commendable person, I'm being dismantled day after day, torn between my own desires and my family's needs. All of my attempts to beautify and adorn my inner life seem futile against the onslaught of daily superficial tasks that eat away at my time and abilities.

Before I had children, I had ambition and talent. I was two years into a Music Performance degree—a promising bassoon student on a full-ride scholarship. But from the time I was a young girl, I also knew that I wanted to be a stay-at-home mother. So when I married at the tender age of twenty, I willingly left behind my musical aspirations and moved with my husband to another state. The music professor who had groomed me as his prize student wrote several letters imploring me not to abandon my musical talent, whatever else happened in my life.

At the time, I didn't understand what motherhood would require of me. Now, years later, I second-guess myself.

Although I readily chose motherhood over finishing my degree, a part of me has never acknowledged the loss of what I might have been, nor come to terms with the cost of my personal sacrifice.

Over the years, I've moved through alternating cycles of personal neglect and nourishment. Sometimes it's just easier to give in and allow my life to become utterly consumed by the menial and trivial than to justify or assert my individual needs. Then, disgusted with my malaise, I rise up, spurred to action by a resurgence of energy, determined to find new ways of incorporating creative expression into my life without upsetting the domestic applecart.

Like a salmon's impulse to swim upstream, the urge to improve my mind and keep my brain stimulated with fresh experiences and challenges seems innate, almost primal. Struggling for my inner life, I know I must keep oxygen flowing through my intellectual gills or I will die. Pushing against stagnation and opposing currents, I swim for mental survival, obsessed with reaching some instinctual goal and preserving my sanity.

* * *

One day in the middle of my identity crisis, I pull the Wonder Mold box down from the cupboard. My eye catches a phrase printed on the side of the box: "Create the doll of your dreams!" I turn the box over slowly in my hands, looking at the photos of the Prom Queen, the Bride, the Mermaid on her seaweed-covered rock. I realize I have forgotten something vitally important: a woman can remake herself in an infinite number of ways.

* * *

Months pass, and I'm sorting mail. I spy a flyer advertising community enrichment classes. As I flip through the pages, my eyes rest on the description of a beginning adult ballet class. My heart flutters hopefully like a butterfly's wings on an airy spring breeze. From the time I was a young girl, I have harbored the secret wish to be a ballet dancer. I want to register for the class, but feel afraid and insecure. I'm thirty-six, far too old to begin ballet now. Then George Eliot's words, "It's never too late to be who you might have been," tease at my thoughts. I pick up the phone and sign up for the eight-week class. I've watched my two daughters dance for years. Now it's my turn.

Giddy with elation, I invite my girls to accompany me to the store to purchase dancewear. As we enter, they immediately rummage through the clothes racks.

"Oooh! This one would look good on you, Mom." My older daughter holds up a plum-colored leotard.

"Will you try that one on, Mommy?" My youngest points to a pink dress with a long, flowing skirt.

Before I can answer either of them, a sales clerk approaches. "Can I help you find something today?" she asks.

"Yes. I need to purchase some ballet slippers," I tell her.

"For your girls?"

"No, for *me*," I assert, answering her puzzled gaze with a wide grin.

After an hour of shopping bliss, we leave the store with my new dancing attire. I can't resist taking the ballet slippers from their box and sniffing the soft pink leather soles. Dreamily, I revel in the smell of expectancy.

Several weeks later, I arrive at the ballet studio for my first lesson. A bell above the door jingles merrily as I walk in. The walls are painted a buttery yellow and are covered with whimsical bric-a-brac. Hesitantly, I follow six other women of varying ages to the back dressing room, where we change into our ballet shoes and dance clothing.

When we return to the dance floor, we are greeted by our instructor, a fresh, energetic young woman named Jenny. She leads us through a warm-up at the barre, instructing us how to properly stretch our bodies. My muscles, taut with stress, begin to relax.

It is good to reach for a dream, I assure myself. Our instructor tells us to breathe in. Air fills my lungs. *It's okay to focus on myself for just this one hour.* I turn inward to the barre.

Just below eye level, resting on a window ledge in front of me, is a framed quote by Martha Graham: "There is a vitality, a life force, an energy, a quickening that is translated through you into action, and because there is only one of you in all of time, this expression is unique. And if you block it, it will never exist through any other medium and it will be lost. The world will not have it."[1] I turn this new thought over in my mind, believing.

*   *   *

After a year of hard work, Jenny informs us that our class will dance in the spring recital. Each week I show my daughters the dance I am learning. Together we practice relevés at the kitchen countertop and piqué turns down the hallway. Between vacuuming and scrubbing toilets, I practice my pirouettes, over and over. Mundane housecleaning chores no longer seem a burden. I am no mere servant girl. I am Cinderella getting ready for the ball.

The evening of the performance, my family waits in the dimly lit auditorium. In a back dressing room, I practice my *tombé, pas de bourrée, glissade, assemblé* combination and hope that years of performing as a musician will help me stay composed now that the moment to prove myself is here. Jenny gathers our class together and leads us backstage where we wait for our turn.

Silently we follow her up a side staircase. Pushing through black stage curtains, abruptly, I am thrust into a dazzling flood of white light. For a brief moment, I'm disoriented, but eventually I find my place onstage. A cool panic seizes my muscles. *The song is only three minutes long,* I reassure myself. *I can do this.*

The music begins, and my frozen muscles begin to thaw. I rely on body memory now, my arms and legs on automatic pilot. As suddenly as it began, the electrifying experience is nearly over. I land my final pirouette, bow to the applauding crowd, and exit the stage, savoring the intoxicating taste of euphoria.

* * *

Two weeks after the recital, I discover I'm pregnant with my fifth child. My ballet instructor encourages me to continue dancing, but deep down I know that having another child will mean relinquishing ballet. I am thrilled to be expecting again, but it nearly breaks my heart to leave behind something I have come to love so much. I savor each remaining lesson, continuing for another three months, until my expanding abdomen makes pliés too difficult and awkward.

The reverence is ending. I curtsy out of respect to the dance and to the body.

As I leave the studio, my hand rests lightly on the doorknob. I take one last look around the room, then turn to see the melancholy autumn wind jostling the faded leaves across the parking lot, prodding them ever forward. When I am ready, I inhale deeply and walk out, knowing I may not return this way again.

*   *   *

Several months later, my daughters and I sit in a darkened theatre at Christmastime watching Act II of *The Nutcracker*. The Sugar Plum Fairy escorts Clara and the Nutcracker to her candy castle where she entertains them with a medley of dancers. Suddenly, a clumsy, towering form is wheeled onto the stage. It is Mother Ginger, an oversized puppet woman atop a gigantic hoop skirt.

The boisterous music starts and, from beneath her skirts, eighteen unruly children pour out. They begin tumbling and skipping around Mother Ginger while her arms wildly flail in the air. Waving and blowing kisses to her children, Mother Ginger beams with matronly pride but is powerless to join them in the farcical dance. After several minutes of their rowdy antics, she beckons to them and, like a mother hen, draws her chicks back under the protection of her skirt. My girls and I laugh and clap as the bonneted contraption is wheeled offstage.

After the performance, my daughters and I walk out into the unseasonably warm winter day. We hold hands, swinging our arms freely as we talk about the flexibility of the Arabian dancer. My unborn son suddenly bends and twines in my womb, a hard knot forming where his tiny heel stretches my flesh to capacity.

"Ouch!" I cry out, instantly releasing my daughters' hands. Drawing my hands upward to caress the sore spot on my belly, the image of the doll cake, restored to wholeness, flashes briefly into my mind. In that moment, I realize how inextricably connected to my maternity are my mind, heart, and hands. I smile, finally accepting that all of these disparate parts, essential to the core of my identity, comprise who I am.

"What are you so happy about, Mama?" my youngest daughter asks as she tucks her hand back into mine.

"All the possibilities," I reply, deftly spinning her outward into a lithe orbit around my promising axis.

NOTE

1. Agnes de Mille, *Martha: The Life and Work of Martha Graham* (New York: Random House, 1991), 264.

Since You Were Born

Darlene Young

Since you were born I've never been alone,
never will be, standing now at zero on a line
that stretches out forever to the right.
Always at the edges of my sight
you pull at me, your dance a haunting grace.
Nevermore I'll live in just one place:
my restless senses stretch like tentacles into
other rooms and lives to protect you.

Since you were born, I've stood upon a cliff,
exposed to gales until I'm stony stiff
with fear, which I disguise as rules or whims
to keep you safe. Humming the hymn
of "all is well" to soothe myself, I stride
ahead. But dizzy with an inward tide,
the wash and pull between "enough" and "should,"
I flinch. Constant atonement, motherhood.

Since you were born there comes sometimes at night
a sense there's something dark that I must fight
without a sword. At night, upon my chest
you and all your children's children rest.

A leaden handicap of dread, of grace.
The future is both straightjacket and brace;
for though I gasp, I must admit the cost
of breath is just: untethered, I'd be lost—

because, since you were born, I've tasted fruit
I never knew could grow from the thin root
of my cold life. I've savored all your grins,
your honeyed sleep, the freshness of your skin—
delicious. This new fruit is more than sweet;
my tongue prickles with terror as I eat.
But even terror lends a tang: it's joy,
since you were born. My son, it tastes like joy.

Making the Grass Greener

Courtney Kendrick

Christmas is the worst time to be infertile. I know; my husband and I have been through four childless Christmases. It's all too easy to fantasize about baby-themed presents, toys, and clothes. I've learned the best thing to do is also the oldest trick in the book: stay busy.

On a frozen December evening, I drove my black car over to visit my brother Jesse and his family in their new home. My sister-in-law Lindsay loved to paint each room with dynamic shades of color. I was most excited to visit the nursery where two-month-old baby Max slept. I'd heard from other family members that his room was the crowning jewel of the house.

Jesse was gone playing city-league basketball when I arrived, so Lindsay gave the tour as four-year-old Lydia and two-year-old Jude scampered around my feet. Lydia pointed out the Christmas tree she decorated—all by herself—and Jude showed off tricks on the vibrant red microfiber couch. The baby slept in his swing, weighed down by heavy cheeks.

And the nursery. Oh, the nursery! Brown with pink high-lights, wood floor and white woodwork. Painted zoo animals on canvas framed about the room. Tiny baby clothes filled the closet: frilly clothes on miniature hangers, crocheted sweaters folded next to white knitted booties. And the rocking chair—all dark wood and soft curved surfaces and hand-carved flowers. It was Jesse's present for Lindsay on her first pregnant Mother's Day.

This was my dream, and she was living it. Not so much the gorgeous house, though it was nice. Not even the perfect nursery—it was nice too. But a Mother's Day with meaning. A real reason to receive a potted plant after sacrament meeting.

It's not like we hadn't tried to achieve the dream: infertility experts, sperm analysis, artificial insemination, clomid, hormones, acupuncture, and magic water tuned to my biofeedback energies. My biological clock ticked to a beat slower than God's will for me. We prayed it would catch up, but in the meantime I had to endure Christmas and Mother's Day empty-handed.

Before I got too emotional, I decided it was best to leave the room. Lydia demanded that I try the lemon drops from the natural foods store; I couldn't say no to lemon drops. We sat at the bar in the kitchen, looking at the perfect shade of gray for the art deco tile. I was *this close* to feeling sorry for myself when my friend heaved a great sigh and said:

"I have to be honest with you." Her voice shook. "This life is so hard! It's *so* hard! I don't know how to do it!"

I started to blurt out something, which was smothered by Lydia's words:

"I haven't been to the store in days, and we're completely out of food! How am I supposed to go to the store with three kids? It's impossible. I could wait for Jesse to get home, but when he is home *I* want to be home, or I'll never see him!"

Recognizing an *Ensign*-type moment to offer service, I said, "Go right now! I'm here. I'll hang out with the kids. I'd love to!" Lydia and I nodded at each other.

"I don't *want* to go to the store, Courtney!" Lindsay walked in circles around the kitchen. "I know you'd do that for me, but I don't *want* to go! Because if I did, I'd get fifteen minutes out that door and my baby would start crying, and I haven't pumped. I couldn't leave you here with a crying baby, and I can't leave a hungry baby! I'd feel guilty all around."

"Take the baby with you!" It's the obvious solution.

"I don't *want* to take the baby! He'd cry with me too, and then I'd have to nurse in some stinky stall at Wal-Mart." She took a deep breath and shook her head. "You have the best life. Sometimes I stay awake at night thinking about it. How nice it would be."

Suddenly Lydia got pushed out the backyard door by Jude, who demanded that *she* needs to go outside. The window pane muffled Lydia's cries of, "IT'S SO COLD OUT

HERE!" which woke up the once-serenely-sleeping baby, who wailed so loud that the swing moved back and forth by the sheer force of decibels.

"See?" Lindsay looked at me square in the eye, justified now that I got to witness the animation of her complaints.

"Okay, so I'll go for you," I suggested. "Just make a list." *They might still take my entry to the* Ensign, I thought.

"No. No, thank you. I just want to complain. It's just hard."

I certainly understood *hard*. I liked talking with someone about the emotional havoc that is infertility, without hearing about their sister-in-law that went to see this doctor in Squaw Valley, New Mexico, who gave her an herb that made her ovulate four times a month and why don't I give the clinic a call? Or without a friend's metaphor that marriage is like college, and you don't get your diploma until you have a child. Or the four-hundredth person to say, "Well, you know, the fastest way to get pregnant is to adopt. My neighbor's son . . ."

Sometimes you don't want an answer or a suggestion or a story. You just want empathy, the impossible task of feeling the same thing as a person whose shoes you haven't tried on.

Lindsay and I had a stalemate. I wasn't about to feel sorry for her—she had babies!—and she couldn't see past my carefree Bohemian lifestyle—my time was my own! There was no point in any further argument.

So after some time spent listening, and then laughing about a few things, I left. It was getting dark, and I thought about going home, but something didn't feel quite right. Had I offered enough service? Did I do all I could for Lindsay? Was there something more I could have done?

And suddenly, I knew what it was: I had to go shopping.

I was gone for hours. I went to clothing stores and food stores, and, of course, Target. I tried on clothes and smelled different cheeses and sang along to the blaring Christmas music. I stopped to talk to acquaintances I ran into and asked them their opinion on gifts. At the grocery store, I waited for the tasting booths to refresh so that I could try the spinach penne pasta and decide for myself. I hung out at music-listening booths and played a Playstation 3 demo. When I got hungry, I went to my favorite restaurant and just sat, enjoying every single bite. And I thought about Lindsay.

I could imagine her putting jammies on Lydia, fishing Jude out of the tub, and promising her swinging baby that she would be "right there" for a nursing session.

If she was going to be envious of my lifestyle, I might as well live it up for her.

And I hoped she'd do the same for me.

Release

Heather Harris Bergevin

Into the wild, you,
brown fur bobbing—
pause,
   scenting revelry;
fragile,
     dart
eyes grasp each
     leafstonepetalnewness
muscles tensed to flee
from danger, to safe cover
You do not peek back at us,
releasing you this early Tuesday,
but we
remember your pulse
quicken, our breath
stop
whisper
go on, go on,
as you
continue the grassy
last steps to school.

Watch with Me

Emily Halverson

Although my mother had seven little ones to love, she made each of us feel like an indulged, only child. Every night she'd come to my bedside with an hourglass in hand and a smile on her face that told me that for the next blessed while, she was all mine. I'd talk about my six-year-old crush on Jedediah Bingham, and she'd rub my back. Only when the final remaining particles of sand had filtered to the bottom of the hourglass did she move on to my sister Mandy. I was convinced that if she could have, she would have remained there all night with me. I'm sure Mandy believed the same about herself, along with the rest of my siblings. I guess convincing others that they were loved was just Mom's gift.

What Mom could never have known, however, was that those filtering sands counted down not only the minutes she had left with us each night, but the numbered days and months she had remaining with us on earth. Cancer would claim her when she was only thirty-six—her oldest child was twelve, her youngest, one.

I was eight.

Although enough time has passed that I'm now a mother myself, truths gleaned from those savored evenings remain.

Life's sand is ever-flowing, but its supply is not unlimited, for the bottom of the hourglass is quickly full. You cannot stop the flow, but you can learn to notice, to touch, and savor each grain that passes.

Have you ever sat down to eat something yummy, only to be distracted by a phone call just as you take your first bite? The next thing you know, the phone call is over, and your food has disappeared. But you don't recall tasting a thing.

* * *

My stomach hurt for the better part of July. As I watched my three towheaded preschoolers on our trampoline—bumping into each other like pinballs and giggling uncontrollably—I often found myself lamenting, *Something special is coming to an end.* I ached along with Robert Frost that nothing gold can stay, and in their childish play I sensed a saffron sunset before me.

My oldest was starting kindergarten in the fall. Life as we all knew it would never be the same again. The transition seemed so unnatural. To go from having all four at home to having my oldest away for eight hours of the day would deeply affect us all. Eden would soon be leaving at seven in the morning, not returning home until after three. There'd be time for a snack, a bike ride, a bath, and some dinner—rushing each of these events to make sure her seven o'clock bedtime was honored, so she'd be rested enough to do it all again the next day. Another eight hours of mothering I'd never get back.

I'd always known that day was coming. An experience I'd had years before had foreshadowed the melancholy of change that motherhood would inevitably bring. Eden and I felt it together, even though she was not yet three. I was rocking her to sleep, singing her usual request, *"Where are you going, my little one, little one? . . . Turn around, and you're grown. Turn around and you're a mother, with babes of your own."*

As I sang those words, my voice thick with emotion, Eden looked up with watery eyes. She held my cheeks in her palms, and with my face in her tiny hands she said, "Mom, that song makes me sad."

"Me too, Eden."

We sat there in the quiet for some time and allowed tears to slip softly down our cheeks, swaying in that third-generation rocking chair and comforting each other with our closeness. For that moment, our souls connected as equals, and we grieved.

But I hadn't spent every moment of Eden's first five years wishing to hold back time. Many days were colored by the paradoxical perspective of not wanting life to change, yet wondering if I could bear its chaos a second longer. I'd wonder how I would make it through the next twelve hours before bedtime arrived, while worrying that those hours would never be enough to harvest all the possible joy.

How could I want to fast-forward, pause, and rewind all in the same breath?

*   *   *

June 18, 2006

For me, the secret of enjoying motherhood is in the moments. To stop and hear the peals of laughter, to touch the tiny hands, to notice the organic smell of their sun-warmed bodies after they come in from playing outside on a hot day—and to be deliberate enough to enjoy it all. Who—when they've slowed down enough and have come outside of themselves enough— could not enjoy a child? This is the surest way I know of enjoying motherhood—ENJOYING my children. Taking the time and learning the skill of being present in the moment.

This is my greatest desire and my greatest anxiety—that it's going too quickly and that I've had too many children too fast, to be able to squeeze all the life and love out of these moments that I can. I feel as though I'm in a race against time to suck all of the joyful marrow out of each stage before it's gone.

I need to ask Madeleine more probing, nonsensical questions so I can hear her creative answers.

Me: So why can't you marry a dinosaur?
Maddie: Because he doesn't have hands.

Me: Oh, [asked innocently and very interested] and he needs hands for you to marry him?

Maddie: Yes [said with absolute surety]—and he only has dinosaur feet.

I need to hold Eden as much as possible before she gets so big that I can't.

I need to hold Jacob's hand for a moment every day so that I never forget the moist pudginess of his fingers and the way his vulnerable little hand feels in mine.

I need to sing him his "homemade" bedtime song about what I see in his eyes every night, *knowing that those nights are numbered.*

There is so much to see, to ask, to notice, to laugh at, to pause and enjoy, to delight in.

I need to capture in words what it's all been like—how it's felt, and how they're changing, and how it's changing me. Immortalizing words that allow me to be "present" in the moment again and again.

* * *

Sometimes the Lord extends a tender mercy not by eliminating a certain trial, but in warning you that it's coming.

When I was fourteen years old, my older brother Brent was released from drug rehabilitation and was home for the first time in years. We'd always been close, and we soon picked up right where we left off—staying up late talking and laughing, understanding and soothing each other's pain. At times we'd talk so late that I could feel my eyelids and spirit losing the battle. How often I wanted to wrap up the moment and doze off into teenage slumber. But something inside warned me that I would not always have him with me.

Could ye not watch with me one hour? (Matthew 26:40.)

I've often wondered about the meaning of the Lord's frequent plea that we *watch*. Watch, for the day is close at hand. Watch, that we enter not into temptation. Watch, so that we are awake, alert, and deliberately aware. The antithesis of distraction.

The Lord had warned me that I should watch with Brent. And thankfully I did.

Not more than a year later, Brent passed away.

* * *

Eden's first week of school came and went, and I was surprised by how joyous this feared transition turned out to be. She'd jump in the car at the end of the day, gushing about her twin-sister friends, Mabel and Edith, or how she'd oil-painted her own version of Van Gogh's *Starry Night*.

If I was so afraid of losing her to kindergarten, why was this next stage so enjoyable? Perhaps because, although life was changing, joy could still be found in my relentless resolve to handle every grain of sand as it passed.

I then understood that my deeper struggle with kinder-garten was not only that Eden was leaving—but the reminder it served that time was passing. Like watching my one-year-old, Christian, teeter around our butterscotch-suede couch. He'll soon be so strong on those legs that he'll spend less and less time in my arms. Or noticing how little Madeleine's dress-up clothes seem much tighter these days—buttons stretched taut, her creamy skin peeking through. And sensing that her days of make-believing she's a bride are only num-bered until the gown she wears is real.

This awareness brings power to my mothering. And change.

One evening after a long day of parenting alone, my aching body and sputtering brain rejoiced as the last child was tucked in. "No more talking, or you're all in big trouble," I called out in warning.

A few seconds passed. I then heard Jacob's little voice. "Mom?"

I sighed loudly and retorted a stiff, "What?" to let him know I wasn't happy.

"Can you come in here and give me some *soft time?*"

Although exhausted, I couldn't help but giggle at his phrase. *Soft time.* He'd never said that before, and I was curi-ous how he'd define it.

"What's soft time?" I asked in careful innocence—

interested and unmocking—not wanting to scare his honesty away by my question.

"When you're lovin' me," he replied simply.

With nowhere to go but up, I pulled my tired body off the couch and sang him "In Your Eyes" one last time. He fell asleep with a contented smile, and I couldn't help but notice how his tanned, five-year-old body nearly filled his bed frame.

Watch, therefore, that ye may be ready. (D&C 50:46.)

Ready for the day when I'll understand that this "one hour" was merely seconds. And so I will try to watch every moment.

The perishable food is before me. I want to taste every bite.

* * *

An object lies on my kitchen counter that makes my stomach roil every time I pass it. A freshly cut, fourteen-inch braid of Eden's golden hair.

It was a practical decision.

With her kindergarten year over and summer upon us, we're spending more time in the pool than out, and shorter hair is simpler. But I can't help feeling like I've lost something irretrievable, like I've somehow severed the past five years of her youth.

Looking at that swatch of hair floods my heart with memories—the lock has suddenly become a symbol of her kindergarten year. How I'd carefully curled it into mermaid waves for her first picture day, and used oriental chopsticks to pull it up into two Princess Leia buns for her international kindergarten program. The times I consoled her tears as I ran a brush through it too quickly during our morning rush. How I taught her to wrap it around her shoulder so that neither of us would sit on it as we snuggled on the couch with *Frog and Toad.*

That yellow braid haunts me for days. I can't stand to look at it, but I can't put it away.

A casual comment from a friend the next day jars me from my melancholy. "Wow, you cut her hair! It's darling, but it's almost like it's not Eden."

Not Eden? *No,* my mind refuses. *Eden is not her hair, some Earth-bound mortal defined by changing details. She's so much more.* I remember again sacred impressions her father, Jared, and I had received the night before Eden was born—that although we would soon be enjoying her presence, countless others on the other side would be mourning their loss.

Not only had she always been Eden, she always would be.

I pull my eyes off the braid and think about my little girl with soft jade eyes and shoulder-length hair in the next room. I feel a surge of joy—genuine comfort only truth can bring. *Eden hasn't gone anywhere, Emily. She's right there. And she will always be. So go be with her!*

Happily, I call her in to join me for a "date" in the kitchen—just her, me, and an overflowing sink. But not before I'm finally able to put her braid away.

Yes, I will watch Eden change. And yet I will watch her remain the same. There is no eternal loss here. There can't be.

A sympathizing friend reminds me of a scientific concept that I've always loved because it seemed so very reasonable— the conservation of mass. That is, matter cannot be created or destroyed, although it may change form. If these past five years I've shared with Eden are not matter, I don't know what is. And if Joseph Smith taught that "the past, the present, and the future were and are with [God]," then maybe somehow all those moments that I've watched—and perhaps even some that I didn't—will be preserved as sweet vapors until time is no more and I begin to experience life as God does. Not life as "back then" or "one day soon," but life as an "eternal 'now.'"[1]

Perhaps watching can be painful at times, because I must acknowledge that time is passing—but not because, once passed, it's forever gone. Just like the sand that slips from the top of the globe to the glass floor below, it is not spilled or lost. It is stored.

My dad has always said that his favorite age for his

children is the one they are at. I like that thought. To me, that is watching with hope.

Watching the change, and seeing what's not changing.

Watching it pass, and knowing it's not leaving.

Tasting every bite, but believing in God's everlasting covenant that the meal never ends. The food is perishable, yes, but there is more to come. And all of it, ingested, becomes a part of me.

NOTE

1. Joseph Smith, *Teachings of the Prophet Joseph Smith,* compiled by Joseph Fielding Smith (Salt Lake City: Deseret Book, 1976), 220.

April 1996

Sharlee Mullins Glenn

Earth rushes up to catch him
      cushions, embraces, then releases
flings him high toward the heavens
so blue
     and blue
          and endless blue

sunlight splashes in his eyes

five springs old
     he wrestles clouds
     swallows butterflies
     bathes in dirt

I watch, entranced
wrist-deep in suds
held hostage by a greasy pot
until a joy (or is it longing?)
so deep and sharp it cuts
releases
sends me bounding
     hands still dripping
out into that place

that vast expanse of time and space
where I can leap and run
and drink the wind
together with my child

We dance
and then with outstretched arms
we touch the sky
residual suds on hands
        and wrists
both his and mine (I shared)
catch the light
break it into a thousand tiny
shimmering rainbows
that pop!
        and then are gone.

About the Authors

Each author is a current or former staff member of *Segullah: Writings by Latter-day Saint Women.*

BROOKE OLSEN BENTON was raised in California, but since graduating from Brigham Young University with a degree in English and a husband on her arm, she has called the mountain west home. Brooke enjoys baking with her kids, playing with her kids, and writing about her kids. For more of their misadventures, visit her at brookebenton.blogspot.com.

HEATHER HARRIS BERGEVIN lives in South Carolina with her long-suffering husband, Noah, their two small children, and fifty bazillion mosquitoes. An avid poet, she is also writing a book of essays on adapting to chronic Lyme disease. Most of her ideas appear in the wee hours of the morning, when she can hear herself think for minutes at a time, and when the only sleepy whining is her own.

JENNIFER BOYACK lives in southern California, where she was raised. She earned a BA in English teaching from Brigham Young University. A week after graduation, she married her best friend, Andrew. Together they have seven children. Most of her days are dedicated to caring for family and the attempt to tame clutter and chaos. Jennifer adores good books, interesting conversation, and tasty food—which explains why she eagerly awaits book club each month.

MELONIE CANNON recently moved to Utah with her husband, Dr. James Uhl, and their four children under age nine. She has a BA in English and Italian literature from the University of Utah and the Universita di Firenze. Melonie received her M.Ed. and taught school before becoming an Army wife and living overseas. She loves to read, write, and try new things.

BRITTNEY POULSEN CARMAN lives in beautiful northern Idaho where she is pursuing a master of fine arts degree in creative nonfiction and teaching composition and creative writing at the University of Idaho. Brittney served a mission to Barcelona, Venezuela. She enjoys motorcycles, making Indian food, and fly-fishing with her four-year-old, Stella Blue.

JOHNNA BENSON CORNETT began writing poetry in 2001 at the encouragement of a friend. A fifth-generation Californian, she lives in Palo Alto with her husband and four children. She's a proud alumnus of UCLA, where she graduated Phi Beta Kappa with a linguistics degree. Johnna enjoys organic cooking and karate and considers any day she rides her bike a good day.

MEGAN AIKELE DAVIES lives in Orem, Utah, with her husband and two young daughters (with hopefully more to come). She has finally landed her dream job—stay-at-home mom. She balances her time between parenting and church callings, and moonlights as a freelance graphic designer. She graduated from Brigham Young University in 2000 with a degree in graphic design, and enjoys art, cooking, and reading.

JUSTINE CLARICE DORTON was raised in the Midwest and now lives in Utah with her husband and five children. She is actively involved in local community affairs, as well as writing. In addition to these, she spends most of her days doing laundry, teaching children, and making her kitchen floor shiny. Someday she would like to leave the kitchen floor dull, not make noodles for lunch, and write a book.

LISA MEADOWS GARFIELD is the mother of six and grandmother of four. She the author of *For Love of a Child: Stories of Adoption* (Agate Lake Publishing, 2005), an award-winning poet, a music teacher, and an avid traveler. She lives on five forested acres in the Pacific Northwest with her family, and loves hiking, trees, strawberries and cream, and sitting in puddles of sun.

SHARLEE MULLINS GLENN lives in Pleasant Grove, Utah, with her husband and five children. She served a mission in Italy and earned a master's degree in humanities from

Brigham Young University, where she taught for a number of years. Her work has appeared in journals as varied as *The Southern Literary Journal, Women's Studies,* and *Ladybug* magazine. She has also published a novel and several picture books for children.

FELICIA HANOSEK, a wannabe survivalist, lives in Central Point, Oregon, with her husband and five children. She served a mission in Marseille, France, studied molecular biology at Brigham Young University, and is currently pursuing an MA in humanities from Cal State University— Dominguez Hills. Felicia enjoys volleyball, Constitutional law, gardening, and all things solar-powered. Despite numerous attempts she is still a Fly-lady flunkie.

EMILY HALVERSON, her husband Jared, and their four children live in Nashville, Tennessee. Emily grew up in Penryn, California (with nine siblings she considers her best friends), graduated from Brigham Young University with a BA in English, and served a mission in France. She spends her days freelance editing, writing, reading, exercising (preferably all of them outdoors) and becoming a Christian through motherhood, which she adores.

LISA HARDMAN recently returned to school to pursue a BA in English after an eighteen-year break. She has been published in *Literary Mama* and the *Highlands Ranch Herald,* and has written numerous resource articles for *FastWeb,* the

Internet's leading scholarship search service. Lisa lives in Highlands Ranch, Colorado, with her husband and five children. Her blog is found at www.brainymama.wordpress.com.

HEATHER HERRICK now resides in New York City, though she was raised in Orem, Utah. She served a mission in Canada and earned a BA in English Education from Brigham Young University. After receiving her degree, she taught middle school English in Texas for three years while her husband completed his graduate acting program. Now she "stays home" with her kids, writes a lot of first drafts, teaches preschool, falls asleep reading, and loves cooking.

COURTNEY KENDRICK is a native of Provo, Utah, where she now resides. After five years of unexplained infertility, Courtney and her husband, Christopher, welcomed a baby boy into the world, convincing her that miracles, after all, have not ceased. Besides writing, she tends to a personal blog (cjanerun.com), nurtures a love affair with Modge Podge, and dabbles in vegetarian cooking.

AILENE LONG was raised in northern California and now lives in Houston, Texas, with her husband and their four children. She served a mission in Finland and graduated from Brigham Young University with a double major in Russian and Spanish. She loves foreign languages, tennis, and long-distance running.

EMILY MILNER lives in Utah with her husband and three children. She served in the Ecuador Guayaquil South mission. She graduated from Brigham Young University with a degree in comparative literature, and hopes to return one day to get a master's in English. Or history. Or Spanish. Or TESOL. Or maybe a law degree . . .

HEATHER OMAN lives in Williamsburg, Virginia, with her husband, her two children, her dog, and a pet ball python. She graduated from George Washington University with an MS in speech language pathology. Heather loves reading, yoga, and growing tomatoes the size of softballs.

MARALISE PETERSEN graduated cum laude from Brigham Young University in humanities and history. She is currently on leave from graduate study at Virginia Commonwealth University in order to follow her husband's international career, which most recently has taken the family to Vienna, Austria. Besides grocery shopping daily, she works as a freelance and fine art photographer and serves as the editor of *Blog Segullah.* She also blogs as the Reluctant Nomad at mlphotodesign.com/blog.

KRISTEN RIDGE lives in Lincoln, Nebraska, with her husband Perry and their two daughters. She graduated from Brigham Young University in 2004 with a degree in English literature and a minor in international development. After internships in South Africa and Ethiopia, she served a mission in Paraguay. Kristen spends her bits and pieces of spare time reading, writing, and keeping rabbits out of her garden.

ANGELA W. SCHULTZ is a born-again Mormon, a wife, and a mother of six. Her hobbies include vacuuming, rotating her food storage, potty training, and homeschooling. She's also really good at laundry. She has a bachelor's degree in English and a master's degree in social work from the University of Utah.

ALLYSON SMITH now calls the Cornbelt home, after thirty years in the mountain west. She lives in South Bend, Indiana, with her husband and their five children. She served a mission in Minnesota and earned a BA in history. Allyson spends the bulk of her time writing non-history and trying to keep the homefront intact.

JOHANNA BUCHERT SMITH was raised in the north woods of Canada without electricity or a phone, and eventually made her way to Utah to attend Brigham Young University. She has a BA in linguistics, dreams of making artisan cheeses, and refuses to let her husband spray chemicals on the lawn. She lives in Pocatello, Idaho, with him and their two children on five weedy, beautiful acres.

KYLIE TURLEY grew up in Cody, Wyoming. She has one BA (political science), one MA (American studies), five kids, one husband, no pets, one house to clean, one garden to grow, and hundreds of unfinished projects to do. She enjoys teaching writing at Brigham Young University and researching Mormon women's history, and has won the Morris Rosenblatt/Charles Redd Center for Western Studies Award, and the Colleen Whitley Scholarly and Creative Works Award.

LANI B. WHITNEY loves having a big yard with climbing trees and with children running around in it. She and her husband, Lance, and five children live in a small southern Idaho town (which they vowed they'd never do) and actually like it. She dreams of picking the last weed out of the flower beds and keeping the laundry done, both to no avail. Most of all, she enjoys kissing the fat, beautiful, flawless skin of babies and toddlers.

DARLENE YOUNG lives in South Jordan, Utah, with her very supportive husband and four sons (even the cat is male). She has a degree in humanities and English Education from Brigham Young University. She currently serves as secretary for the Association for Mormon Letters and has published in *Segullah, Dialogue,* and *Irreantum.* She likes to read, sing, knit, eat chocolate, and do yoga (although not all at the same time—except for the chocolate part). She dreams of returning to school for an MFA.

MELISSA YOUNG is a native of Utah and currently resides in Smithfield with her husband and four children. She graduated from Brigham Young University with a degree in communication studies and a music minor. She loves to dabble, and consequently knows a little about a lot of things but not a whole lot about anything.

KATHRYN LYNARD SOPER is a mother of seven children, teenage to toddler. She is editor-in-chief of *Segullah: Writings by Latter-day Saint Women* (www.segullah.org), and editor of *Gifts: Mothers Reflect on How Children with Down Syndrome Enrich Their Lives* (Woodbine House, 2007). Her memoir, *The Year My Son and I Were Born,* will be released by the Globe Pequot Press in March 2009. Her website is kathrynlynardsoper.com.